# CHRIS
# COUNSELING
# AND
# DELIVERANCE

# RAYMOND PRIMUS

Mustard Seed Ministries
Raymond Primus
239 Oak Hill Dr.
Southbury, CT 06488
(203) 264-2361

# CONTENTS

# iNCRODUCCiON

Throughout the course of human history man has struggled with emotional and spiritual problems. As soon as two people were on the face of the Earth the problems began. Adam ate from the forbidden tree and blamed it on Eve. Cain was jealous of Abel and killed him. Our emotions and sin nature open us to a myriad of problems. Psychologists have attempted to find a cure for our problems but for the most part they have failed. They have devised hundreds of theories each claiming that their method of dealing with the human condition is the best way to solve our mental and emotional problems. Freudians claim that their method is the best. Behaviorists state that they have the answers while Jung claims that his method is best. Each discipline thinks that they have found the secret to the soul but unfortunately all their efforts are to no avail. Movie stars go to the top psychologists in the world, often on a daily basis for years, and after twenty years of analysis they commit suicide.

The reason why psychologists are unsuccessful is because the problems that their clients have are spiritual and have to be dealt with on a spiritual level. The Scriptures contain all the answers to every problem we may have in our lives. Hosea tells us that God's people are destroyed for a lack of knowledge (Hosea 4:6). It is up to us to search the Scriptures to identify the problem areas of our lives and find Biblical solutions for them. This book is intended to help you become free to be all that God has called you to be, to be delivered of demonic influences, to be clear of mind, pure in deed, and to have the proper motives for all that you say and do.

# ᴆᴇLiᴠᴇRᴀɲᴄᴇ

The Bible tells us that Jesus cast demons out of people almost everywhere He went. It says that He cast demons out of many people (Mark 1: 34). When He sent the apostles out He gave them authority over all demons and diseases (Luke 9: 1). If it was necessary for Jesus and the disciples to cast out demons, surely it is important for us to do so today. Demons have not disappeared from the face of the Earth but are alive and working evil today. Jesus tells us that these signs will follow believers … "In my name they will drive out demons; they will speak with new tongues; … they will place their hands on sick people and they will get well" (Mark 16: 17).

Many of our problems are demonic. We spend a lot of time and money going to psychologists to find peace of mind and to doctors for what we think are physical problems. The truth may be that some of these problems are spiritual ones.

I have seen numerous cases of cancer, M.S., chronic pain, nervous conditions, and a whole host of other things healed by an hour or two of deliverance. It's a shame that many of our churches do not believe in or administer deliverance. "— my people are destroyed from lack of knowledge." (Hosea 4: 6)

*A $200 a day heroin addict was in his second day of cold-turkey withdrawal. His symptoms were vomiting, pain in his whole body, shaking, coldness, and more. After forty-five minutes of casting out the demons of each symptom as well as the spirit of heroin addiction, he was immediately set free and feeling fine. For the next two weeks he was on fire for God. He was in church almost every night and praising God all day long. There were no more symptoms of withdrawal and no desire for heroin.*

*A seventeen year old boy was diagnosed with brain cancer. The doctors said he only had a 50% chance of living. We did two sessions of deliverance where he felt things leaving him. When the doctors operated on him a few days later they were amazed when they found no cancer!*

*(Also read on pages 78-79 about the deliverance of a young doctor who had cancer in both breasts.)*

Some churches teach that a Christian cannot have a demon. I have done deliverance on hundreds of Christians and some of them have even been pastors and elders. When asked by a Greek woman to cast a demon out of her young daughter, Jesus said that deliverance was not for the unsaved … that deliverance was the bread of the children of God. She begged Him. He relented and cast the demon out of her daughter (Mark 7: 24-30). Scripture also tells us that if you cast a demon out of someone that it can come back seven times worse if the person is unrepentant. Why would anyone take a chance casting demons out of an unsaved person knowing that unless that person then receives Jesus he will be more demonized than before?!

In the Bible it says that seven demons came out of Mary Magdalene (Luke 8: 2). Another time the demons left with a loud shout. If they could tell then that demons were leaving we should also be able to tell today when they are leaving. Assume for a minute that you led someone to Christ that had demons. Wouldn't the demons have to leave at the moment of salvation if Christians were not able to host demons? And if they did leave, surely you would be able to tell that they were leaving. I have seen thousands of people come to the Lord, yet I have never seen a manifestation of demons leave when a person said the Sinner's Prayer. I have and do, however, see manifestations of demons leaving saved people when I call them out in the name of Jesus!

How do you know if you have a demon? Demons come into people only if they have a legal right. There are four ways they can come into a person.

1.  **Generational curses:** God allows demons to enter in the fetus to bring about the same sins of the father (Exodus 20: 4).
2.  **Sin:** When you sin you give the devil a home … or a place to the devil (Ephesians 4: 25-27).
3.  **Soul ties:** The demons dwell in your flesh and when you become one flesh with someone demons are allowed to transfer into you.
4.  **Transference of spirits:** We lay hands on people for the Holy Spirit for healing, for gifting and for ordaining ministers. If the Holy Spirit is given through the laying on of hands so also could demons be transmitted the same way. We do not lay hands on people for this very reason when we administer deliverance.

How do you know if you have a demon? If you have habits or addictions that you have to struggle to control (if you can control it at all). If you have unrelenting thoughts or if you have a disease it may be demonic in origin. If you have strong urges to sin, if you can feel them (especially at night) or if you hear voices then you may have a demon. Most people need deliverance since demons can enter us when we sin … and who hasn't sinned?

How do you cast them out? Just repeat, *"I cast out the spirit of _____ (name the sin or disease) in the name of Jesus."* Repeat this over and over for about five minutes. By this time the person should start to yawn, cough, burp, or feel them leave. Sometimes, it feels like claws sticking in you and the person yells in pain. Sometimes the person can feel them moving inside of them, often from their stomach and up their throat. When this happens they sometimes get stuck near the Adam's apple and the person may not be able to talk for a while.

Mark: 16 states that in His name (Jesus) they will cast out demons. You don't have to plead the blood or sprinkle holy water on the person or quote scriptures at the demons. You need not say anything other than "I command you to leave in the name of Jesus." Also you don't have to yell at them or get mad when they don't leave right away. They won't leave any quicker because you can yell real loud. When you get mad at them at lose your temper you just look stupid. I never raise my voice above a soft tone and those demons come out by the hundreds! You can sprinkle in a few other phrases while casting the demons out like " come out by the authority given to me by Jesus Christ" or "You cannot resist the name of Jesus, you must leave now".

So many times I have taught people how to cast out demons. I will tell them to say exactly what I say..."In the name of Jesus..." When I finally let them finish the deliverance many people will say everything except what I just told them! I don't know why they will avoid saying the only thing that will cast them out.

Read the story about Jesus and the demon possessed man. (Mark 5: 1-20). Jesus commanded the spirit to leave the man but they didn't leave him right away! The demons begged Jesus over and over to allow them to go into the pigs. They didn't come out until Jesus relented and allowed them to do so. Even Jesus had to argue with the demons before they came out. Don't think because you just command them once they will leave. If, however, after five minutes of calling them out with nothing happening you probably will have to break generational curses, soul ties, or have the person repent of unforgiveness. For a more detailed teaching on deliverance I strongly recommend the book, "Pigs in the Parlor," by Frank Hammond.

*A 17 year old girl was tormented with panic attacks, she had to be pulled out of school twice or more a week because of this irrational fear. She couldn't leave the house and avoided public gatherings. Her life was going to be ruined because of these attacks since she would be unable to go to college or find work. Her Mother brought her to me for deliverance.*

4

*It is important to find the root cause of any demonic activity, this girl never had anything traumatic happen to her in her life. I determined that she had a generational curse of panic attacks since both her mother and father and sister suffered to a lesser extent in the same way. I broke the generational curses and spent three hours a week for the next six weeks casting out spirits of fear and panic. I would cast out the spirit of fear of crowds, then the spirit of fear of getting sick in public...I cast out a spirit for every manifestation of her condition.*

*After the first week she went off all of her psychotropic drugs and stopped seeing her Psychologist. She told him that he or the drugs weren't able to help her after years of treatment but what I was doing was setting her free. He told her she would die without his help! There was only small improvements over the first several weeks but by the fifth week she was doing fine. We agreed the next meeting would be the last one that she needed and it was! Within weeks she graduated from high school, attended the graduation, sang in church in front of the whole congregation, got her driver's license, hangs around with her friends so much her parents never see her anymore and is now in College hundreds of miles away from home!*

Don't let demons ruin your life or the lives of people you know!

One final warning: the demons will try anything to keep you from getting deliverance. You must make this a priority in your life. Three women in a six month period were suffering from severe pain from auto-immune diseases. After one hour of deliverance all three were pain-free for the first time in years. I told them that they needed more deliverance in order to keep their healing. Not one returned and all three lost their healings! GET DELIVERANCE NOW. DON'T LET THE DEVIL RUIN YOUR LIFE!

# CURSES

The Bible talks about curses over a hundred times. Surely something that is mentioned so often in the Scriptures has to be of profound importance to us. Curses affect our lives in so many ways they can alter our health, finances, relationships and even our time of death. They come upon us in a number of ways. Some of them are listed below.

1. **Generational curses**: The children are punished for the sins of the father for three and four generations. (See the end of this chapter for more on generational curses.)

2. **Cursing yourself**: The words we speak have power. When we say negative things demons are sent to bring about these things. We have all said something like, "I can never do this," or "I'm no good and I'll never be able to stop this time," or "I'll never get married," or "I'll be poor the rest of my life." These are all curses and come about because of your spoken words.

*A friend of mine tells the story of a man he knows who saw a nice truck go by and said, "I'd give my right arm for a truck like that." Six months later he was able to buy a truck like the one he had seen. Within two weeks he got into an accident while driving his new truck and lost his right arm!!*

3. **Curses spoken by others:** People can curse you just by speaking out negative things. Witches and Voodoo practitioners can put a curse on you that can dramatically affect your life.

4. **Curse of the Law:** (Galatians 3: 10) "Cursed is everyone who does not continue to do everything written in the Book of the Law." If you are trying to earn your salvation by being "good enough" to get to Heaven you are under a curse because this scripture says that clearly no one is justified by keeping the law.

5. **Curse of dishonoring your parents**: Deuteronomy 5: 7-10 states that if you honor your parents you will have a long life and things will go well with you. This is a blessing. Yet, if you don't honor them then a curse is placed on you and you may not live a long life and things may not go well for you.

6. **Cursed objects:** Deuteronomy 7: 25-26 states that if you bring a cursed object into your home you will be accursed like it. People do not look at something and say, "Look at this cursed object. I'd like to have that hanging on my wall." Cursed objects are often works of art.

*A friend was going bankrupt and was desperately trying to sell his house. A year went by and nobody was even looking at it anymore (it was during a major downturn in the real estate market). Whenever I visited I would point out all the cursed objects in his home. He had statues of gargoyles three feet high greeting you at the door, an ivory statue of "Moses" except he had horns and a trident (pitch fork), Moslem prayers hanging on the wall, Mexican death masks on the other wall, and unicorns all over the place (they are mythical creatures not created by God and have supernatural powers). Finally one night his wife was convinced by the Holy Spirit and she threw everything in the trash. At 7 A.M. the next day her real estate agent called her and said she had someone who wanted to see the house right away. A deposit was put on the house that very morning. The cursed objects were keeping the house from being sold!*

7. **We are under a curse when we make judgments.** See the chapter, "Judgments."

8. **A father, spiritual leader, or other authority figure can give a blessing — or a curse**. These words have more power than curses spoken by others. Your father might have said that you're no good and that you will never amount to anything. That is a powerful curse because of the authority bestowed on him by God.

9. **If you break a vow to God you could be under a curse.** See the chapter, "Vows."

10. **If you have unforgiveness you are under a curse.** See the chapter, "Forgiveness." Tormentors will be sent to torment you if you don't forgive everyone of everything they've done.

11. **Pride is a curse.** God says that He resists the proud.

## MORE ON GENERATIONAL CURSES

We all know that children tend to take after their parents not only in looks and body type but also in personality and even in health problems. We conclude that it is because of genes but genes aren't always the answer. Deuteronomy 5: 7-10 tells us that the children will be punished for the sins of the fathers for three or four generations. This means that demonic spirits are assigned to bring about the same sin in the children as the parents.

I have always had a problem with a loving God punishing an innocent child for their parents' sins until my fifteen year old daughter moved in with me. To that point she was living with her mother and I was seeing her on weekends. We always had fun and never ran into any problems, but the day she moved into my house she tried to take over. She would order me around telling me to wash the dishes or clean up. Every day I would tell her, "I'm the parent, you're the child. I tell you what to do, you don't tell me." After six months or so I was so fed up with her behavior I blurted out, "You're the most egotistical, self-centered, rebellious, prideful, arrogant person I ever met." At that moment I heard the Holy Spirit say to me, "Yes, just like you." I was shocked! My daughter had all the personality traits that I had but I always justified my sins and thought that these "minor" faults were "cute." Now I could see myself like others saw me and I didn't like it. So God puts the same sins of the parents on the children so that we can look at our children as if they were a mirror and see ourselves as we really are. Then we can repent and help our children overcome their sin.

Generational curses not only affect our sin life but also allow sickness and addictions to pass along to our children. We see certain ailments running in families. These are curses that can and should be broken. Cancer, heart disease and a whole host of other problems can be from generational curses. When breaking a curse it is important to cast out the demonic spirit assigned to bring the curse about. It must be repeated over and over until the person feels that the spirit is gone.

Once a very close friend of mine brought someone he knew for deliverance. I spent fifteen minutes trying to cast out spirits to no avail. Then my friend told me that God told him that the man had a "vagabond" spirit. I tried for five minutes to get this one out but nothing happened. Next my friend told me that God gave him Psalm 109. I read it out loud. It says about the wicked, "Let his children be continual vagabonds and beg: ...." Before I finished reading the man started coughing, belching, and having all kinds of demonic manifestations. He was set free from everything that we had tried to cast out before. The demons had a legal right to stay until we broke the generational curse.

Another reason why God punishes the children for the sins of the father is because many parents know and accept the fact they will be punished for their own sins but when they realize that their beloved children will be punished they may not sin.

Another more obscure reason is that when Adam sinned we (all of humanity) suffered the consequences of that sin. "Consequently, just as the result of one trespass was condemnation for all men, so also the result of one act of righteousness was justification that brings life for all men" (Romans 5: 18). In other words because of Adam's sin we all became sinners partaking in his sin (likewise because of Jesus' act of righteousness we can all take part in his holiness). So when our fathers sinned he carried our seed in him and we became partakers of his sin. When Adam sinned he carried the genetic code for the entire human race. Each of us was present in him when he fell.

I often thought that it was unfair that I should be punished for Adam's sin. That is until one day the Lord asked me if I would have sinned if it was me in the garden. I said, "Of course not!" Then He said to me, "Then why do you sin now?" I had to agree with the Lord that if I were in the garden I would have done the same as Adam (as hard as that is to believe).

10

So generational sins are curses in our lives that predispose us to certain sins. Our lives are affected on a daily basis by these curses. Often we try to overcome a sin area only to keep falling into the same temptation.

**Remedy:** Galatians 3: 10-13

> [10]*All who rely on observing the law are under a curse, for it is written: "Cursed is everyone who does not continue to do everything written in the Book of the Law."*
> [11]*Clearly no one is justified before God by the law, because, "The righteous will live by faith."*
> [12]*The law is not based on faith; on the contrary, "The man who does these things will live by them."*
> [13]*Christ redeemed us from the curse of the law by becoming a curse for us, for it is written: "Cursed is everyone who is hung on a tree."*

So all who rely on observing the Law are under a curse and everyone who does not continue to do everything written in the Book of the Law is cursed (vs. 10). Clearly, no one is justified before God by the Law because, "… the righteous will live by faith." Christ redeemed us from the curse of the Law by becoming a curse for us, for it is written: "Cursed is everyone who is hung on a tree."

So, everyone who tries to get to Heaven by obeying the Ten Commandments is under a curse. You would have to obey all of them throughout your entire life and no one could do that. Paul tells us that there is a curse in the law and that we are all under it. But Christ redeemed us from the curse by becoming a curse for us by hanging on the cross.

Just as Jesus took the sins of the world on the cross He also took our curses on the cross. But, just as our sins aren't forgiven unless we confess them and apply the work of the cross — Jesus having paid the death penalty for our sins — so too, our curses are not broken from us until we identify them, confess them, and apply the work of the cross to them.

A simple prayer to break a generational curse would be …
**"Heavenly Father, I break the generational curse of lust that was**

*passed down from my father to me. Jesus took that curse on the cross and I am now set free from that curse that would cause me to lust. I command all demons that have been assigned to bring this curse about in my life to leave me now in the name of Jesus."*

When the curse is broken you may see remarkable changes in your life. The power of that sin in your life is often times completely broken. On the other hand sometimes there is little discernible change. When a curse is broken it is like arm wrestling; when you are under a curse the enemy has you down an inch from the table and you must struggle with all your might to keep from being defeated. When the curse is broken it restores you to an upright position. Sooner or later you will realize that you no longer have to fall into that sin anymore. You might have problems for a while because you are in a habit of sinning and habits are often both physical and spiritual. Sometimes you may also fail because your faith in the power of your prayer is weak and you may have to repeat it until your faith level is stronger. You may also fail at first because your mind needs renewing. As long as you think of yourself as a smoker you will have a difficult time resisting that temptation.

**Biblical references**: Exodus 20: 5

> *⁵You shall not bow down to them or worship them; for I, the LORD your God, am a jealous God, punishing the children for the sin of the fathers to the third and fourth generation of those who hate me...*

# soul ties

The Bible tells us that when two people get married they become one flesh (Mark 10: 6-9). This might seem to be untrue since there is no physical difference between the two people before and after they take their vows. So why would the Bible say something that is so obviously untrue? There must be something that happens when people get married in the spiritual realm that we can't see. It is a spiritual connection that connects the two people. This bond is formed not only at the time of marriage but the Bible also says that if you have sex with a prostitute you become one with her and unite her with the body of Christ (I Corinthians 6: 15-20). We call these bonds "soul ties." They connect the flesh of two people in a spiritual way that allows spiritual things to transfer from one to the other.

There are other ways that soul ties form. In the book of Samuel it states that Jonathan so loved David that he became "knit in the soul" with him. This is the same Hebrew phrase for when a man marries a woman he is to "... cleave to his wife; and they will be one flesh."

Just how does a soul tie affect a person? By becoming one flesh with a person you are now subject to having the demons that dwell in that person's flesh transfer into you. You may have thoughts about that person that won't go away or you may dream about them or be

13

tempted in sins that they are partaking in that you never were tempted in before. You may have the same thought that they have and say the same thing at the same time. You may also know things that are happening to that person even though you are not near them.

Some examples of good soul ties are husband and wife, mother and child, identical twins, close friends, brothers and sisters. These relationships can be good and healthy but they also may be bad. If you have an abusive parent you will form a soul tie with them that can haunt you for the rest of your life.

Examples of bad soul ties are teen idols (the children start acting like their rock star idol), an abusive boss or teacher, a hypnotist, sex partners outside of marriage, a spouse you had sex with before marriage, a person you are fantasizing about, a person who is using witchcraft on you and people you are sinning with. You can have a good or a bad soul tie with people such as a pastor depending on his control over you and your submission to him. Whenever you submit your will to someone (a parent, boss, pastor, friend, etc.) in an ongoing relationship a bad soul tie can form. An example of a soul tie forming by submitting to someone may be when you go to a hypnotist. You tell him that your will is not strong enough to stop smoking so you allow him to put his will upon you. He now can control you with a post hypnotic suggestion. When you have a soul tie that person may be able to control you without you even knowing it.

When I first learned about soul ties I decided I was going to break those connections with all the women that I had previously, before Christ, had sexual relations with. So one morning as I was taking a shower I prayed to break all of those bonds. Fifteen seconds after I broke the last one the phone rang. I ran out of the shower, dripping wet, wondering who would be calling me so early in the morning. It was my future ex-wife. She had left me a year before and had only called me twice during that time to yell at me. This time, however, she was nice to me and asked me to do her a favor. I gladly agreed (since I was trying to win her back), but I noticed that her voice sounded scratchy. I asked her if she had a cold and she said no, but that she had just awakened and wanted to call me before I left for work. She had to have started dialing the phone the very second I broke the last soul tie.

She knew there was something different about me and she, therefore, was able to be pleasant for the first time in a year. There was one girl in particular (an ex-girlfriend) that my ex-wife had been jealous of. She must have sensed that the tie between me and her had been broken.

Sometimes when we are doing deliverance with a person a demon will not come out because we have not broken the soul tie with the person that allowed that demon to come in.

**Remedy:** Hebrews 4: 12

> [12] *For the word of God is living and active. Sharper than any double-edged sword, it penetrates even to dividing soul and spirit, joints and marrow; it judges the thoughts and attitudes of the heart.*

So repent of the sexual sin (or idolizing, submitting to false authority, over-loving or over-dependence of a person, etc.) and say, ***"In the name of Jesus I break the soul tie between _____ and me."*** Repeat that with everyone you have a soul tie with. Sometimes in a strong tie you must break the tie in the three parts of your soul. You should repeat it for your will, your emotions and your intellect.

# Rejection

Jesus was rejected of men (Isaiah 53: 3) yet He loved and forgave them. We all suffer rejection, even me! I can't believe that people would reject me I'm so cute. But they do, boy do they! It hurts so much to be rejected especially by people that we love. Many of us have been rejected by our parents ... or at least we feel that we have because they didn't meet our expectations. How does one recover from knowing that your own mother doesn't want you? What about people who have been rejected by their husbands or wives, boyfriends and girlfriends? How about people who have been so rejected that nobody ever even wanted them to be their boyfriend or girlfriend!

We tend to get our self-worth from what other people think of us. If we are popular then we feel good about ourselves but if nobody wants to be around us we often feel that we are worthless. We cannot use other people as a barometer for who we are. Hitler, for most of his reign, was the most popular man in Germany. There will always be people who will reject us. Sometimes we will have the approval of everybody but then one person says something negative to us and we are crushed. Or we ignore the critical person (who is right) and listen to the people who dote on us. If we let rejection take root it will affect everything in our lives.

**Remedy:** Repent of the sin of idolatry — we make what others think of us more important than what God says about us. We should hold fast to who we are in Christ and not what we are in the flesh. We want to respond to rejection as Christ did, with love and forgiveness. If people who reject us are more important than God's acceptance then we are in big trouble ... and who isn't. Cast out the spirit of rejection!

**Memorize and believe these scriptures:**

- **There is now no condemnation for those who are in Christ Jesus ... (Romans 8: 1)**
- **He will love you and bless you ... (Deuteronomy 7: 13)**
- **... I have loved you with an everlasting love; I have drawn you with loving kindness. (Jeremiah 31:3)**
- **The Lord God is with you, He is mighty to save. He will take great delight in you, He will quiet you with His love, He will rejoice over you with singing. (Zephania 3: 17)**
- **Because of His great love for us, God, who is rich in mercy, made us alive with Christ even when we were dead in transgressions ... (Ephesians 2: 4)**
- **This is love, not that we loved God, but that He loved us ... (1 John 4: 10)**
- **And so we know and rely on the love God has for us. God is love ... (1 John 4: 16)**

# FEAR OF REJECTION

To avoid the pain of rejection we sometimes alter our normal behavior and personality to escape further rejection. A person may exhibit multiple personalities, changing who he is in order to please the person he is with at the moment. We all do this to a certain extent. A mother acts differently towards her children than to her boss. It could become a problem when it is carried out just to avoid rejection. When we put aside our personality and take on another it may allow a demonic spirit to take over and form another personality. If a young girl has been rejected by an abusive father, as an adult woman she may revert to a little girl personality when she is around her dad and act in such a way as to avoid further rejection. We tend to adapt to keep from being hurt by rejection.

If you have a fear of rejection you need to know first, that fear is not of the Lord! It comes from the devil who is a liar. Whatever the devil tells you will be a lie and if it is a lie then the opposite is true! We are told to meditate on the Word of God day and night. Instead we often meditate on the words of Satan day and night. He tells us we are going to fail, that we are no good, and that people hate us and have done bad things to us. If you know it is the devil that is telling you these things (and he probably is) then it is a lie and the opposite is true. It's almost like getting a direct word from God.

When we have experienced rejection we tend to build walls to protect us from further rejection. We don't allow people (or God) to get close to us. Our walls don't work, though, and they actually bring about more rejection. Anytime we respond to a situation in a way contrary to what God wants it always leads to more of the same problem. When we put up walls people reject us all the more. We also wall in all the hurt so that it never gets healed. It is like a cut that scabs over without being cleaned first. The germs grow and cause an abscess that could end up killing you. And so it is with spiritual wounds. If you put up walls around spiritual wounds you have walled in the demons and trapped them …. they will now torment you.

**Remedy:** You must allow the Holy Spirit to break down the walls you have erected to protect you. Find the cornerstones — perhaps bitterness, anger, hatred, or hurt. Sometimes it helps to visualize the power of the Holy Spirit knocking down these walls. Repent of the bitterness and anger (or other sins) and watch the dynamite of God crumble the walls down. Be willing to be vulnerable again and let God be your defender. Do not defend yourself. Let people back into your life but lower your expectations. Cast out the demons of hurt, anger, fear of rejection and others. Determine that you will not alter your personality just to avoid rejection (if this was a demonic problem). The mark of a mature Christian is that he will not be swayed by the opinions of others just to gain acceptance. On the night that Jesus was arrested Peter denied Him three times. He altered his behavior and his beliefs to suit others.

# juɒgmeṇɕs

Matthew 7: 1-2

> *¹Do not judge, or you too will be judged.*
> *²For in the same way you judge others, you will be judged, and with the measure you use, it will be measured to you.*

When we judge people we put ourselves in a position where God must now judge us. If we are harsh and strict in our judgments, then God will be harsh when he judges us. One of the biggest sins the Pharisees committed was that of being hypocrites. They judged everyone according to their rigid standards, yet they failed in the bigger things of mercy and love. Jesus told them that they were devils and that they were going to Hell. Imagine, these were the most religious people of the time — perhaps all time. They had the right scriptures, they tithed on everything they had, they prayed long and loud, they were in church all the time … and yet they failed to measure up to the Lord's standards. Because of their harsh judgments of others they were judged by their own standards.

When Jimmy Swaggart and Jim Bakker fell into sin I judged them hard. I said, "How could men of God do such despicable things? They deserve to be thrown out of the ministry and never let back in again. How dare them!" As soon as I spoke these things my wife corrected me, telling me not to judge them because that would put me into a dangerous situation with God. I quickly repented. I realized that I had nothing to gain by judging them but a lot to lose. What benefit is it to me to speak and think ill of these people? Jesus said if you so much as look at a woman lustfully you have already committed adultery with her in your heart (Matthew 5: 27-28). Am I any better than Swaggert and Bakker in the eyes of the Lord? If I think I am and pronounce judgment on them then judgment must also come upon me. Meanwhile, if I love them and try to restore them into relationship with God without being judgmental God will bless me and not judge me as harshly as I deserve when I fall into sin. So if you have judged people it is wise to repent.

**Remedy:** Repent of making judgments. Get deliverance for a judgmental spirit. Stop thinking negative thoughts about people … or yourself.

Remember that mercy is not getting something that we deserve. Grace is getting something we do not deserve.

Pray, *"God, have mercy on me and those who have offended me even though neither I nor they deserve it. Give us the grace to keep from this sin in our lives."*

# ƒORGIVENESS

One of the biggest problems most people have is the inability to forgive. When the disciples asked Jesus how they should pray He said to pray like this … "Our Father … forgive us our debts as we also have forgiven our debtors …" (Matthew 6: 9-14) Jesus thought it was so important to forgive that He incorporated it into the prayer that millions have prayed on a daily basis for thousands of years.

But, you may say, "How can I forgive him after what he did to me?" Or, "I forgave him but he keeps on doing the same thing over and over so I can't forgive him anymore." How many times must we forgive somebody? Peter asked Jesus that same question. He said, "Lord, how many times shall I forgive my brother when he sins against me? Up to seven times?" Jesus said to him, "I tell you, not seven times; but seventy-seven times" (Matthew 18: 21-22). In other words, you must always forgive someone. Now that doesn't mean that you have to be stupid. Let's say you hire a babysitter and he molests your child. Do you have to hire him again? NO! You would call the police and have him arrested. But in your heart you must have forgiveness towards him. Why, you might ask …

Jesus tells a story (Matthew 18: 21-35) about a man who was forgiven a gigantic debt by his master but then went to another man

22

who owed *him* a very small debt and demanded payment. This man couldn't pay him at that moment so he was sent to jail until he was able to pay. When the first man's master heard of this he sent the man to prison to be harassed by tormentors until he also repaid *his* debt. These tormentors are also sent to us to torment us until we forgive everyone who has done anything to us. These tormentors are demonic spirits that steal our peace, our sleep, and make us angry, etc.

Forgiveness does not mean you have to be a doormat. You may attempt to keep yourself from being hurt by the same person over and over. But God does not want you to carry these hurts and negative feelings for the rest of your life.

How do you know if you truly have forgiven a person? It is when you can think upon the incident that hurt you and not have the pain associated with the hurt or any negative feelings towards that person. You really have forgiven when you feel love towards your enemy! It can happen … and it should happen all the time. It's up to you. Unforgiveness only hurts you and keeps you from a closer relationship with God. Don't you want peace in your life? Don't you want happiness and joy? Then don't let that *creep* continue to steal it from you. It's bad enough that you got hurt once but it's silly to carry that hurt forever, giving the person the power to hurt you every day even though he's not even in your life anymore.

Many years ago God told me to leave the church that I was going to so that I could help a much smaller church of the same denomination grow. I didn't want to leave my church but God convinced me with signs and wonders. I told my pastor that God said that I would know when I got there if this really had been Him speaking to me. My pastor gave me his blessing and said I should go and see. What I found was amazing! God confirmed His Word in a powerful way. My pastor then commanded me not to leave his church. I told him that I was going to follow what God was instructing me to do. He then told my wife that she was not allowed to leave his church — that I was demon possessed, that I was not saved and never had been! He said I was in sin because I left his church and that she was to now be the spiritual head of our home. She was not to listen to anything I said. She had just had our baby two months before and was suffering from postpartum depression. This put her into an even deeper depression. This pastor continued to counsel her in this way for several months until she decided to leave me.

This man cost me my marriage. In the divorce hearing I lost $400,000 and was left on the brink of bankruptcy. I lost all of my friends and my reputation. My daughter was now a thousand miles away and my wife made it impossible for me to have any kind of relationship with her. In other words this pastor was largely responsible for me losing everything I worked for in my entire life. I lost my lovely wife (who never mentioned divorce until after she left), my child, my reputation, and all of my friends (who were members of his church). If anybody had a reason to be angry it was me. But, I knew that God wanted me to forgive this pastor. For the next two weeks after my wife left I would repeat over and over that I forgave him. I didn't feel any forgiveness and I heard a lot of "yeah buts." I determined that this man was not going to steal my joy. It took two weeks before I really felt in my heart that I had forgiven him. When his name came to my mind I started to feel love towards him instead of anger. Here are the steps I used to find forgiveness for him — don't listen to the "yeah buts" or entertain any negative thoughts towards the person.

### How to forgive:
1.  Choose to forgive the person. It's a decision and a command from God. He wouldn't command you to do something you didn't have a choice in.
2.  Ask to be forgiven for having unforgiveness. Your unforgiveness is just as much a sin as whatever that person has done to you.
3.  Forgive God for allowing that situation to occur. God is in control of the entire universe and nothing can happen without his permission. If you are mad at God you're in big trouble. Repent quickly; He loves you.
4.  Bless the person who hurt you. Hope that good things come his way even in the ways he hurt you. Ask God to bless him with prosperity, with a faithful mate, with good health, etc.
5.  Free him from any debt he owes you. You're probably not going to get it anyways. Don't hope that God 'gets' him. Don't

hope that justice be done. You are not the judge ... leave that to God. The Lord says that vengeance belongs to Him.

6. Ask God to heal the wounds you have and to heal the person who hurt you. Many times people cannot help but hurt others because of the pain *they* harbor. Ask God to restore the relationship in a healthy way.

7. Thank God for the situations that hurt you ... "And we know that in all things God works for the good of those who love him ..." (Romans 8: 28). God won't allow anything to happen to you that He can't turn around for good. But you must believe that God can and will do it otherwise He won't — without faith it's impossible to please God.

8. Be delivered of unforgiveness and bitterness!

# ChE POWER OF OUR WORD

Words have power! When we pray angels are sent to answer our prayers (Daniel 10: 10). When we say negative things demons are sent to bring those words into effect. We all know that if we tell a child often enough that he is bad and will never amount to anything, this will probably be the case. We also know that a positive attitude increases our chances for success and a negative one often brings failure. The words we speak are important.

I do think that many people get carried away with this teaching and ignore the truth. They speak things that are untrue just because they are trying to be positive. For example, a person I know was dying of cancer and only had a few months to live. When I would ask her how she was she would say, "I am healed." She would never respond with the truth because she said that would give the disease more power over her and that her words would heal her. Well, words don't heal — Jesus does! I think that she should have replied in a more truthful way, perhaps saying that she was still fighting the disease and was continuing to pray that God would heal her ... and then ask for prayer for a full recovery.

If you feel God has promised you something (such as healing, prosperity, relationships, etc.), hold fast to it, speak it out and remind yourself of the promise and faithfulness of God's Word. Be careful, however, of looking like a fool. The world is watching us and when we say that God is going to do something you better be right. If we want our unsaved friends to come to the truth, how can they believe us about salvation when the other things we tell them about God don't come true? It may be better to say, "I *feel* that God will do this."

Nobody likes to be around people who are negative, but I also don't like to be around people who believe that everything they say with their mouths will come to pass. I've seen this doctrine fail most of the time. In the case of the woman dying of cancer ... when she died four of her closest friends dropped out of the church. They were so sure they had heard from God that she was healed and they were devastated that *their* faith had not healed her.

Some people teach that no matter what disease you have, you have already been healed and all you have to do is claim it. I believe that you should seek a healing until you have a manifestation that the healing has occurred (or at least you felt the disease start to diminish through prayer.) Sometimes a healing could come from any believer (Mark 16: 17). Sometimes it may only come through a person gifted in that area (1Corinthians 12), or only through an elder (James 5: 14). Sometimes God gives health to you spontaneously! In any case, when you have a manifestation of the healing, claim it and hold fast to your healing. Speak it out and don't let the devil steal it.

# vows

Make your vows to the Lord and keep them (Psalm 76: 11)! We expect the Lord to keep His word, and we often quote Scriptures at Him, reminding Him that He promised to prosper us, to keep us from harm, to bless us, to answer our prayers, etc. How can we expect God to remain faithful to His word if we aren't faithful to our word? We make promises to God and never keep them. "I promise to go to church every Sunday, Lord … if you give me enough money to pay my mortgage." Or, "I promise I'll never do that sin again." Sometimes we say silly things like, "I'll be damned if I ever forgive him." Our word has power and we must be careful what we say and what vows we make to God or even to one another. When you borrow money and promise to pay it back (even to Master Card) God expects you to do what you promised. If you promise to do something for your husband or your kids you must do it. There is an old saying that says a man's word is his bond. A bond is a guarantee that something is going to be performed. Today most people do not keep their word. We have trouble believing anybody, even our political and religious leaders. Our parents have not kept their word nor have our children. Who can we trust? Only God! But, it should not be like that. We, as Christians, must be an example to the world that we are different.

What happens if you don't keep your vows?

*There is a story of a man who was called by God into the ministry just before WWII began. He resisted the call and ran from God. One day years later he found himself on a life raft in the middle of the North Sea. The ship he was on was sunk by the enemy and chances of being rescued were nil. Being about as desperate as a man can get he called out to God. "Lord, I promise I will serve you in the ministry if you rescue me." Shortly thereafter, a miracle occurred. He was picked up and brought back to safety. After the war the man did not keep his vow to the Lord. His life was miserable and he soon found himself on the streets living like a bum.*

*Years passed until he remembered his vow to the Lord. He was now willing to fulfill the call on his life. Once again he called out to God telling Him he was ready to do whatever He wanted. A door of opportunity was opened to him and he became a preacher. His life was now wonderful and for once he had peace with God.*

If you have made promises to God or to others, you are expected to make good on them. Ask God to show you what you must do to make your word good. This could be a great opportunity to demonstrate the true Christian life. It may even be the start of bringing those people you have disappointed to the Lord.

**Remedy:** Repent of those vows that you have not kept. Ask God to set you free from them and be careful not to make vows that you might not be able to keep.

# ƒALSE EXPECTATiONS

A false expectation is any expectation that does not come true. When we expect something to happen and it doesn't or when we expect a person to do something and they don't, that is a false expectation. Most of our anger comes from having false expectations. How do you know if you have a false expectation? Are you angry about something? Most likely you expected something different to happen and when it didn't, you got angry.

The first time I gave this teaching a lady in the group told me that her husband came home from work every day and left a trail of clothing from the front door to his bedroom and she had to pick it up every day. I asked her how that had made her feel. She said it made her angry. I told her that she had a false expectation that her husband would be neater with his dirty clothing. She said, "But, he *should* pick up his own dirty clothing or at least not leave them throughout the house." I replied that it didn't matter what he should or shouldn't do, the fact remained that she expected him to do something that he was not doing. Again she said, "But he should!" I asked her how long this had been going on and she said it had been about twenty years. I then asked her, "You've been mad at him for twenty years?" She answered, "Yes, every day for twenty years I've been mad at him for leaving his clothes all around the house." So I instructed her to "lower your expectations" as her husband was not going to change and she was going to have to pick up his clothes anyway. If she expected *that* then at least she wouldn't be angry. Again she responded with what he *should* do. I finally told her that she was going to die an angry old woman.

Expectations are arbitrary. We can set them anywhere we want. You can expect your child to get all A's or all C's. If your expectations are set too high and your child gets one B you will be disappointed and you will be angry. Meanwhile, if you expect him to get all B's and he does better than you expected you will rejoice!

Some of us are angry at God because our lives didn't turn out the way we expected. Perhaps a loved one died or we are suffering from a terrible disease. We may have been disappointed with God for not answering our prayers the way *we* wanted them answered.

Being angry with God is a dangerous place to be. Repent quickly! God loves you and wants the best for you. If things are not going the way you expected, perhaps you are under a curse or you may be in sin. One thing for sure is that "God works all things together for good for those who love Him and are called according to His purpose" (Romans 8: 28).

**Remedy:** Lower your expectations to match up with reality. Forgive and don't judge those who do not meet your expectations.

# NEEDS AND DESIRES

God has given us a desire for approval, for food, sex, comfort, love, etc. When these desires are not met they can turn into needs. The difference between a need and a desire can best be shown when a person first tries heroin. He really likes it and the next day he desires to do it again but doesn't have any money … it is no big deal, so far. When he becomes addicted, however, it is a different story. Now this is a need and he will do anything to meet that need. Needs never are completely fulfilled. They may be temporarily satisfied but soon the need becomes as demanding as before. The heroin addict never gets enough heroin that he says, "Wow that was so satisfying and felt so good I will never need any more."

When our desires turn into needs we do abnormal things in order to meet our needs. The addict will steal and maybe kill to meet his need. We may make fools of ourselves in order to get attention if we have a need for attention (we see that in children who will act out just to get attention — even negative attention is better to them than no attention at all.) A young lady may hang onto her boyfriend's leg begging him not to leave her if she has a need to be loved. The sad thing is that when we have a need it never gets fulfilled and we end up getting just the opposite of what our actual need was.

1.  When you *need* approval from people ... you do things that look so needy that you get rejection instead.
2.  When you *need* appreciation from people ... you do things for everybody and people then expect it from you. Now they take you for granted and overburden you.
3.  When you *need* to be loved by people ... you do things you would normally not do to get this love. Girls will have sex with boys to try and get them to love them; boys will stalk girls and say stupid things to them to get their attention only to be rejected. When you have a need for love you end up getting only conditional love. The boy only "loves" you as long as he wants to go to bed with you.
4.  When you *need* to be needed by people ... you end up getting false burdens. People will just use you and not really need you.
5.  When you *need* sympathy from people ... you look and act pathetic and end up alone. People do not want to be around someone who is always in need of sympathy. These people will suck the life out of you.
6.  When you *need* attention from people ... you will do silly or stupid things to get attention (i.e., class clown) but instead of getting positive attention you get ridiculed and laughed at. People lose respect for you and instead of getting attention you get rejection.

**Remedy:** Recognize your needs for what they are. Realize that the methods you have been trying to meet these needs with have not been working. Ask God to turn your needs back into desires. Get deliverance for your needs. Realize that God can meet every need that you have. Repent of the sin of idolatry (looking for man to meet your needs instead of God). Be convinced that God's love for you is more important than man's love for you.

# Love is a choice

All emotions follow decisions that we make. If we decide that a situation is dangerous our mind causes adrenalin to be released ... our body then feels the fear. If we think happy thoughts then endorphins are released and our body feels good and at peace. If we think about a loved one chemicals are released to make us feel a longing for them or a warm feeling. If we think about how a person has hurt us and we are unforgiving, other chemicals are released ... some of these chemicals can cause damage to our bodies ... unforgiveness can cause arthritis, rebellious thoughts can cause cancer, worrisome thoughts can cause ulcers, and fear can cause heart attacks.

The Bible commands us to love our neighbor, to love our wives, and to love our enemies. God wouldn't command us to do something that we didn't have a choice in. Therefore, love is a decision. We have to choose to love a person. Ever wonder why you fall in love with the type of person that you do? Often it is because we made a choice to love them. We may not have made a conscious decision to do so but some time in your life you did. Most little girls tell their dad (even if they are not the best dad in the world) that they love him and want to

34

marry him. Most boys do the same with their moms. We decide at a very early age who we are going to fall in love with and marry. Studies have been done that show that 70% of all people marry someone who is like their opposite sex parent. Your brain pathways are mostly formed during your first five years of your life. Your basic personality is in place and many of the choices you will be making in the future are going to be at least partially determined by the experiences you have had so far ... parents, do not put your kids into daycare before the age of five and let someone else form your child.

So, if we are commanded to love our enemy (or our spouse) just how do we do it? Some of you have tried and failed. Let me help. Perhaps this time you will be more successful.

Read the story about the pastor in the chapter on "Forgiveness." He cost me everything. First I had to choose to forgive him and after going through all the steps I was finally able to do it. Next I chose to love him. After making the decision I refused to think any negative thoughts about him. Every time I thought of his name I would think of something nice about him and when I heard the "yeah buts" in my mind I said, "No yeah buts. I am going to love him." In a short time I did feel real love for him. When I thought of him a warm feeling came over me.

I've seen a number of marriages that were failing badly. Either one or both partners hated the other one. Often, in just one counseling session, the marriage would turn around and the two people would be like newlyweds. So choose to love the people in your life and be happy. Stop looking at your spouse's shortcomings and look only at their good points. If you dwell on their faults you will never be happy with anybody because we all have faults and we will until the day we die. Even if they changed everything that bothers you now, you would soon see other areas that they needed to work on. Who wants to live with someone who always finds fault with you?

# PERFORMANCE

We are taught as little children that when we do good things we get praise and love. When we do bad things we get punished and rejected. So from an early age some of us start to perform to earn love and acceptance. We think that it is what we *do* that will make people love us. To a great extent this is true but sometimes some people can spend their entire lives doing things to get love and they never really get what they are striving for.

Some people try so hard to be loved. And even if they are loved they strive to get love from everybody. They end up performing and doing things to earn love. They usually over-extend themselves and never spend any time taking care of themselves or doing things to make their lives happy. Most comedians did not receive love during their childhood. The laughter and applause of the audience temporarily fulfills their need for love.

**Remedy:** Realize that your value is not in what you *do* but in who you *are*. God made you just the way you are. He loves the fat, ugly, tall, short, and skinny. He has no regard for what anyone looks like or how intelligent they are. He is interested in their character and their nature.

If you are trying very hard to *earn* love you are defeating yourself. Repent of the "idolatry of people" and be happy that God loves you. When we say we can't be happy unless "so and so" loves us we are putting a person's love above God's. How sick is that? Stop performing to get love. It never works anyway!

Stop thinking that God cannot love you because you have sin in your life. You will always have sin in your life! Even if you get set free from your current failures you will not be perfect. God will reveal other areas that you need to work on.

Jesus told us that we must come to God as little children. I try to think of my relationship with God as if I were a two-year old child. Two-year old kids say 'no' to their parents, they spill things on the rug, break things and soil their pants. Yet, the parents still love them! They don't say to the child, "You messed in your pants again! I don't love you anymore!" They know that two-year old children are not perfect. God knows that we are not perfect, that we will sin and say 'no' to Him, however, He still loves us … unconditionally. You do not have to perform to perfection to earn His love.

# mind sets

Sometimes the problems we have in life are because of the way we think. Men do not think like women (if you have not discovered this yet you lead a sheltered life). Children think differently than adults. People who have been abused think differently from people who have had a happy past.

The Pharisees had a mind set that overlooked the miracles of Jesus because they were done on the Sabbath (Matthew 12: 9-14). Their mind set was that the Messiah would never break their laws — a sinner could not be the Messiah. Because they have a faulty mind set they missed salvation and killed the Savior!

Whenever two people disagree each one thinks that he is right and the other person is wrong. The law of averages tells us that we are wrong 50% of the time. We can't always be right. The problem comes because we don't recognize when what we think is right is actually wrong.

When we disagree, instead of both sides digging in and insisting that they are right, a better attitude would be to try and see it from the other person's perspective. Don't just insist that the other guy must change. Try to be teachable. Do not be quarrelsome but be kindly to everyone (II Timothy 2: 24).

I have been asked why God made men and women so differently. Men are usually, I think, more logical and women are more emotional. This difference usually causes strife in our relationships and marriages. The father tends to discipline very strictly and the mother more compassionately. The wife wants to shop and the father wants to save … or spend money on his own toys. These different mind sets often cause marriages to fail.

God made Adam out of the earth, but He took a rib out of Adam to make Eve. Why didn't He make Eve out of the earth also? Because His plan was to take something out of the man that only a woman could replace.

We should look at the difference between men and women as a good thing. We should meld our differences together to form the perfect human, led by logic, but filled with compassion. The two shall become one.

**Remedy:** Repent of mind sets and stop thinking that you are always right. Strive to see the other person's point of view. Would you rather be "right" or "righteous?" God has given you the "mind of Christ" — use it! His ways are not our ways so when you think you are right examine what the Lord has to say in His word, and you will probably find He says the opposite. Ask yourself, "What would Jesus do?"

# YOUR VALUE

Almost every woman I've ever met struggles with low self-esteem. Conversely most men suffer with pride. Why is this so? There are many reasons. To start with, a woman has to be perfect in every body part in order to feel worthy in this society. A woman may have feelings of unworthiness if her hair isn't perfect or her face isn't pretty enough or her shoulders are too broad (or not broad enough hence shoulder pads), her breasts are too large, too small, too droopy, too this or too that, or if she is too skinny, too fat, too flabby, too tall, too short, her legs are too skinny, or she has fat thighs, her complexion isn't just right or a thousand other things like intelligence, personality, posture, etc., that may not be considered perfect. How can anybody try and live up to all of these standards? Women look at themselves in the mirror and see all of their imperfections. Even the most beautiful girls I've known feel that they are ugly.

In this society girls have been the second class citizens compared to men (who have most of the really important jobs). But even with the great strides women have made in this area they still feel inferior. Girls perform better in school than boys, yet girls still don't think highly of themselves.

I look at ten year old girls and they seem filled with self-confidence and have high self-esteem. But something happens to them when they reach puberty. Perhaps it's hormones. We all know when a woman has PMS her self worth sinks to new depths.

Perhaps the most important thing that contributes to a woman's self-worth is her relationship with her father. For a girl this is the most important relationship in her life. It affects who she chooses for a mate, her value system, her self-esteem, her happiness, her career choices and a whole host of other areas of her life.

If a girl's father is abusive and not loving she usually is not going to feel good about herself. Women need the love and approval that only their real father can give. Unfortunately, most fathers are not even in the same home as their children (only 23% of children are living with both of their biological parents).

Girls are also competitive with each other so they tend to judge each other harshly as to physical looks. Even girls who are popular with boys soon find out what the boys really want — sex — and this makes a girl feel like a sex object rather than valued as a person. Even though moms try to give positive messages to their daughters, it doesn't make up for the lack of love and affirmation by their dads.

*There was a man who was told by Jesus to go into a warehouse to pick out a vase. There were thousands to choose from. Some were painted so beautifully, some were of gold, and some were made of silver. Some of them had to be worth a fortune. Others, however, were plain and drab. A number of them had major flaws in them and some were so ugly even a beggar wouldn't have chosen them.*

*The man took his time in selecting the one vase that he could keep for himself. Each vase was sealed at the top so he couldn't see if there was anything inside. After considerable thought he finally chose a vase that was weather-beaten and looked to have little or no value. By far it was neither the most beautiful nor the largest. When Jesus asked him why he chose that particular vase the man replied that this one had character. He could tell that the people who had owned it put it to good use and the weathering showed that it was strong and would not just fall apart if it was misused. The Lord smiled and told the man that he had chosen well. Jesus opened the vase and inside was a fortune in diamonds! The value of the vase was not in how it looked on the outside but by what was on the inside.*

Even if you feel that you are the worst sinner in the world (as Paul thought he was), inside of you resides a treasure that is more valuable to God than you can ever imagine. Your treasure is your willingness to love and obey your Creator. Decide to do that now and don't let the enemy lie to you and tell you that you are worthless anymore!

Be like the vase that the man chose. Be a person who can weather the storms of life, who can be well used without breaking or falling apart. Your beauty (or lack of it) has nothing to do with your worth to God. He is like the expectant mother who prays to have a perfect baby but when the child is born with a major birth defect, the mother tends to love that child more than her other children. Even though we have major defects in our lives, God still love us! You deserve His love!

Many people suffering from auto-immune diseases have such low self worth they feel that they deserve to always be in pain. Two ladies with M.S., several with Fibromyalgia, and a few others with similar diseases were recently healed with just one deliverance session. They were all told that they could lose their healing if they did not return for more deliverance for their self-hatred. None of them returned and they all lost their healing!

# OCCULC PRACCICES

In the book of Deuteronomy, God commands us not to practice divination, soothsaying, and sorcery or to be a medium or a wizard or to communicate with the dead. God says whoever does these things is an abomination to the Lord. (Deuteronomy 18: 10-12)

Some of the problems in our life could be because we participated in occult practices. There is a curse on you if you have ever participated in the following practices:

1. astrology (even just following your horoscope);
2. mediums;
3. fortune tellers;
4. Ouija boards;
5. tarot cards;
6. mind reading;
7. ESP;
8. eastern religions;
9. martial arts;
10. false religions;

11. automatic handwriting;

12. palm reading.

Most of these practices are bad because they seek to guide your life instead of God. The practice that most people question me about is martial arts. The reason why it was included is because most martial arts are based on the eastern religious practices. They require you to bow to the "master." The bowing is to the divinity they believe dwells in that man.

They also often teach that there are supernatural conduits of power within the body and you must learn to focus these powers.

Usually the teacher will be a believer in a New Age religion and some of their students will become converts.

The last reason is because they are teaching you to hit, kick and hurt people. They might tell you this is for self defense but when you are teaching eight-year old boys how to hurt people I doubt if they will differentiate to only use it in self defense. Jesus told us to turn the other cheek, not to hit back!

**Remedy:** You must repent of your involvement with these practices and turn away from ever doing them again. Don't follow the leading that they have given you … they are directions from the devil. You may also need deliverance from these as they allow demons to enter when you engage in the occult.

# SOWING AND REAPING

Some of the problems we have in life may be from the seeds we have sown throughout our lives.

Galatians 6:7-9

> [7]*Do not be deceived: God cannot be mocked. A man reaps what he sows.*
>
> [8]*The one who sows to please his sinful nature, from that nature will reap destruction; the one who sows to please the Spirit, from the Spirit will reap eternal life.*
>
> [9]*Let us not become weary in doing good, for at the proper time we will reap a harvest if we do not give up.*

I have a friend who became a Christian in his late 30's. He had led a life of sin — sex, drugs, adultery, and every kind of perversion known to man. Three years after his conversion he complained that he had served God with his whole heart, he had given thousands of dollars to the Church, led people to the Lord and basically did everything he was supposed to do and yet his life was still miserable. His marriage was on the rocks, his kids ill-behaved, and he was out of a job and going bankrupt. He said this "sowing and reaping" doesn't work. I told him, "Sure it does, you're still reaping everything you've sown for the last thirty years." The Bible says that "in due time" you shall get your reward "if you don't lose heart." Five years later his life improved, his marriage and finances were better and his kids became better behaved. He is just now starting to reap the good things.

A word of caution about this subject ... most TV preachers teach the prosperity message. They say, "If you give money you will be rich and God will reward you a hundred fold." This teaching is sick! I've known thousands of Christians and I don't know of any that got rich this way ... except the preachers who are soaking the poor for their last dollar. Does God really want you rich? Jesus said that it is harder for a rich man to enter into the Kingdom of God than for a camel to go through the eye of a needle! He also said that where your riches are that is where your heart will be. The early Christians were not interested in getting rich but rather sold everything and laid it at the Apostles' feet (Acts 4:32-37).

I do believe that God promises to meet your needs ... that you will not starve or go homeless. Jesus said to pray "give us this day our daily bread." If you were rich you would never have to pray that prayer. He wants you to be dependent on Him for everything every day. The book of James tells us that we have not for we ask not and when we ask, we ask amiss to consume it upon the lusts of the flesh. In other words we may suffer because we don't ask God for a blessing and then when we do pray for something we ask for things that won't be good for us.

God has made me wealthy, though. I believe I am one of the few Christians who did get wealthy that wouldn't have without supernatural blessing. I think the reason for this financial blessing is because whenever God blesses me with a sum of money I put it into the Kingdom. I gave up a large income and purchased three Christian book stores — not a good place to earn a living. But because I seek first the Kingdom of God, He has prospered me through other financial means and "He has added all these things unto me." I do not seek money. As my soul prospers, God prospers me.

# STUBBORNNESS

We must have a heart willing to serve God; yielded to Him and ready to learn. We cannot be unteachable, thinking that we know everything there is to know about God. God judges our hearts.

II Chronicles 30: 8-9

> [8] *Do not be stiff-necked, as our fathers were; submit to the Lord. Come to the sanctuary, which he has consecrated forever. Serve the Lord your God, so that his fierce anger will turn away from you.*
> [9] *If you return to the Lord, then your brothers and your children will be shown compassion by their captors and will come back to this land, for the Lord your God is gracious and compassionate. He will not turn his face from you if you return to him.*

It's so refreshing to have someone come into my ministry and ask to be taught everything I know about God. They have a hunger for knowing Him. They don't argue Scriptures but just soak in everything the Lord has to say. These people grow so fast in the Lord that I'm amazed. You should be like that! I'm not saying to blindly follow someone but if what he has will bring you closer to God then get as much as you can!

Many people are stuck in their religious traditions that they were taught as a child. I've heard many Catholics say that they were born a Catholic and they are going to die a Catholic. They don't want to know the truth and they are not willing to learn more about God. They think they have all the truth there is and are unwilling to search for more (the same can be said for all denominations … the Baptists as well as other denominations can be just as "stiff-necked"). If you were born into a family of Satanists would you still insist on dying a Satanist? Almost no one converts to Catholicism unless they have to for marriage reasons. It's almost impossible to convert Jehovah Witnesses because of their "stiff-necks." So be teachable and study the Word to show yourself approved. Put aside what man has taught you in the past and don't be like the fathers in Chronicles.

When I was a brand new Christian I devoured the Bible day and night. My fear was that my zeal for learning was so great that soon I would know everything there was to know about Christianity. After all, there was only one book to study, the Bible. In college I could master a text book in three months. I was afraid that I would master the Bible and then become bored with Christianity.

Well, it's been over twenty years and almost every time I read the Bible I learn something new! So … be teachable. If you are open to learn everything that God has for you and you are not stubborn you will grow to be a great Christian!

# your mind

There is a battle going on for control of your mind. Whoever controls your thought controls you. The devil is an expert at getting us to focus in on what he wants us to think. The Bible tells us that *every* thought is not our own.

When the devil tempts you it sounds like your own thoughts. The same is true when God speaks to you … your conscience is often the Spirit of God convicting you. So how do you know when your thoughts come from God, the devil, or it is your own thoughts? I John 4: 1-3 tells us that we are to test the spirits. If the spirit does not confess that Jesus has come in the flesh then that spirit is not of God. So to practice hearing from God, ask the spirit, "Should I sin?" You will hear a "yes" or a "no" in your mind. Then ask, "Did Jesus come in the flesh?" Once again you will hear a "yes" or a "no." If it is God speaking to you He will tell you not to sin and that, yes, Jesus came in the flesh. Sometimes people will get the opposite results. Then you know that the devil is speaking to you. In that case ask the same questions again. This time you will get the correct answers. Some people get "yes," "no," "yes," "no," "yes," "no." They need deliverance.

We are told to meditate on the Word of God day and night but instead we meditate on Satan's words day and night. He tells us we are no good, we are going to fail, we can't do anything right, bad things are going to happen to us, etc. We think the devil's thoughts all day and all night. God on the other hand tells us to think on these things "whatever is true, whatever is honorable, whatever is just, whatever is pure, whatever is lovely, whatever is gracious ..." (Philippians 4: 8). Don't think those negative thoughts any more. We are commanded to renew our minds and to have the mind of Christ. We are to rejoice in our tribulations and to give thanks for our sufferings. Instead of trying to escape our trials give thanks for them because God is working something good in you. Roman 8: 28 says, "And we know that in all things God works for the good of those who love him, who have been called according to his purpose." So if God is going to do something good with your trial why are you so upset? If you choose not to respond with faith in God and allow your circumstances to get you down He won't be able to turn your trial for good. Without faith it is impossible to please God. If you do not respond properly you will have to repeat the trial over and over again!

The Bible tells us to take every thought captive. In the past a bad thought would come into my head and I would say, "I'm not going to think that," but it would go away for a few seconds and then just come right back again, over and over. I would try not to think the bad thought but I had little success. Then I remembered that I'm supposed to take the thought captive. So I closed my eyes and imagined that I was grabbing that thought with my hand and holding it until I made the thought confess that Jesus is Lord! Then the thought disappeared and didn't come back. I held it captive.

Discipline your mind as an athlete does his body. An athlete will often train many hours every day for years to achieve his goal. People who are into fitness do the same thing. Yet most of us spend little or no time training our minds. We should spend hours a day thinking on the Word of God!

# BE LED BY THE SPIRIT

Jesus tells us that He is going to send the Holy Spirit to us to comfort us, to guide us and to teach us all things (John 14: 15-17, 26). After you receive the Holy Spirit (with the evidence of speaking in tongues) His job is to guide you, lead you, and teach you. You must, however, seek Him and give Him an opportunity to do so. We tend to talk to God, the Father, and to Jesus, but many of us never talk to the Holy Spirit. He is just as much God as Jesus is. He has an intellect ... He will teach you. He has emotions ... do not grieve the Holy Spirit. He also has His own will (John 16: 13) and yearns to communicate with us. Benny Hinn wrote a book called <u>Good Morning Holy Spirit</u> where he teaches us to treat the Holy Spirit as a real live being that is living within us. What a revelation of God!

Romans 8: 14 states, "... because those who are led by the Spirit of God are sons of God." Our lives should be guided not by what we think is best for us but by the Spirit of God. How do we know what the Spirit is saying to us? Ask Him! He will communicate with your mind. It will sound like your own thoughts but that's how God speaks to us. For those who would like to prophesy, speak in tongues and pray for the interpretation. Then listen and you will get a few words in English. Say those few words … you won't get anything more until you say those words … then keep on talking in English without thinking as you do when speaking in tongues.

Remember to always test the spirit (I John 4: 1-3). See the chapter, "Your Mind."

# APPENDIX

---

**This is an outline that can be used for teachings on the basic fundamentals of salvation, deliverance and the Christian walk in accordance with the Word of God.**

# I.  SALVATION

(John 3: 1-8)
Nicodemus, a religious leader of Israel, came to Jesus knowing he was sent from God. Jesus told him that you must be "born again" in order to enter the Kingdom of God. Nicodemus didn't understand this term (do you?) Jesus explained further that a man must be born of the water (flesh) and the spirit. How does your spirit get born?

(John 3: 16-21)
Jesus said that anyone who believes in Him will not be condemned. Why does just believing in Jesus save you? What if you are a horrible person? Could Hitler be saved?
(Romans 3: 21-26)

We are told here that all fall short of the glory of God, but we are FREELY justified by his grace. Justified means justice has been served. Grace is unmerited favor, getting something we don't deserve. Mercy is not getting something we do deserve. Christ redeemed us (which means that he paid the price to get us back … like when you redeem your soda bottles and get your money back) from the punishment of the law. The penalty for sin is death (Romans 6: 23) but the GIFT of God is eternal life. Gifts are given freely; you can't be good enough to earn it.

So what we have is a bunch of disobedient people who deserve the death penalty. Jesus paid that death penalty for us and if we accept that then we don't have to suffer judgment for our sins. God loves us so much that while we were still sinners, Christ died for us.

> *A twenty-one year old girl who was arrested for speeding went before the judge. He asked her how she pleaded … guilty, or not guilty? She pleaded guilty and the judge imposed the prescribed penalty, a hundred dollars or ten days in jail. She said that she didn't have any money and the courtroom eagerly waited to see if this young girl was really going to jail. The judge took off his robes, got off the bench, and paid her fine. Now the courtroom was abuzz. People were thinking that, hey, maybe he'll pay my fine too! The judge put his robes back on and told the people, "That is my daughter, I love her very much. But what kind of judge would I be if I let the people I love off, 'scott-free.' I have to judge everybody the same no matter how I feel about them. But nothing says that I can't pay the fine for her."*

Now, this girl was twenty one years old. She could have said, "No dad I'll go to jail; I don't accept your offer to pay my fine. I'll do it my way."

If you haven't figured it out yet, the judge is God. He is a righteous judge and has to find each of us guilty for our sins and impose the death penalty. But nothing says that He can't come down Himself

(Jesus) and pay the price for us. If we accept that we become His children.

Many people when asked if they think they are going to Heaven they say they think so (or hope so). When asked why they reply that they are pretty good people, they never killed anyone and live pretty good lives.

Let's say that God is in the room with you right now and says, "There is only one thing I don't want you to do; please don't spit on the floor." What do you think God would do if right in front of His face you immediately spit on the floor? Can you imagine disobeying God right to His face! Surely He would smite you one.

Or, let's say that you are in Heaven waiting in line for judgment. Those who have less than a thousand sins are allowed into Heaven and everybody else is thrown into Hell. The guy in front of you has 999 sins and God says, "Wow, you just made it in. You are good enough to get into Heaven." You're next. God looks into the Book of Life and says, "I'm sorry you have a thousand sins and I have to send you to Hell." Wouldn't you say to God, "But I only have one more sin than the last guy. Are you going to send me to Hell for one little sin?" Now God has a problem; it doesn't seem fair to send someone to Hell just because of one little white lie more than the last guy ... so let's say He lets him in. Now the guy behind you has a thousand and one sins and he says to God, "You let the last guy in with a thousand sins. Are you going to send me to Hell because I have one little white lie more than him?" God has another problem and lets him in. The next guy has a thousand and TWO sins ... get the point? Pretty soon Hitler is saying, "But I only have one more sin than Genghis Khan!"

The point is, yes, you do get sent to Hell for one little sin. But it's not the thousandth sin ... it's the first sin. Spitting on the floor is just as big a sin as murder in God's eyes. All sin is punishable by death.

So if we just receive Jesus as our Savior and believe that He died for our sins do we get to Heaven? Well, probably not! You must also make him your Lord (Romans 10: 9). This means that you are going to seek His will for your life and obey Him. You will never be perfect in this life but God is going to judge your heart not your deeds. Paul says that he still does the things he shouldn't and that he is the chief sinner!

By making Jesus the Lord of our lives and the Savior of our souls we become "born again." Our spirit comes alive and we are now able to be in tune with God. How do you know if you have been born again? When you first receive Jesus as your Lord and Savior you are born in the spirit as an infant. As time passes you should be able to look back and see that you are different than what you were before. Every six months you can look back and say, "I am growing more and more like Christ." There may be times when there is no growth and that doesn't mean you're not saved. It only means that you are not taking full advantage of what God has to offer you.

So, if you haven't done it already ask Jesus into your heart. Thank Him for paying the penalty for your sins. Seek His will for your life. Allow the Holy Spirit to search you and show you what sin you need to be set free from. Then make Christ the Lord of your life and obey Him. If you fail it's OK. There are earthly consequences for your sin but you will still earn you way into Heaven, not by what you do but by what God did for you. Now, we obey God not because we fear Him but because we love Him and want to please Him. It is not because we are trying to earn our salvation but because it was given to us as a free gift. It's almost too good to be true! Christianity is different from every other religion in the world. All other religions say that it is what you *do* that earns favor with God. Reincarnation says that you keep coming back until you reach perfection. Jews and others think that you have to be good enough to get into Heaven. True Christianity says that it is what God did for *you* that gets you into Heaven, not what *you* do for God. Our righteousness is like filthy rags to God.

# II.  BAPTISM OF THE HOLY SPIRIT

(Acts 1: 4, 5)
Jesus told His disciples not to leave Jerusalem until they received the Holy Spirit. He told them there was *something* called the "Baptism of the Holy Spirit".

(Acts 1: 8)
Jesus told them they would receive power when the Holy Spirit came upon them.

(John 14: 15-17)
Jesus said that He would send the Holy Spirit to be a counselor, to teach them the truth (vs. 26), to comfort them, and to guide them.  He told them they knew the Holy Spirit for He dwells with them, but sometime in the future the Holy Spirit would be *in* them.

(Acts 2: 1-4)
On the day of Pentecost the Holy Spirit was given to the disciples and as soon as they received the Spirit they spoke in tongues (a language they had never learned).

(Acts 2: 14-18)
The power of the Holy Spirit was so strong that the disciples were staggering, falling down, speaking in tongues and laughing.  The Jews thought they were drunk!  Peter answered them with what was prophesied by Joel: "In the last days, God says, I will pour out my Spirit on all people." If Peter thought that those were the last days then surely we are still in the last days.  Some people teach that the gifts of the Holy Spirit are no longer in existence.  But in verses 38-39 Peter goes on and states that the gift of the Holy Spirit is for every one that God calls.

(Acts 8: 14-19)
The next time the Bible records someone receiving the Holy Spirit is when Peter and John prayed for the new believers in Samaria.  It says

that they were baptized in the name of Jesus but had not yet received the Holy Spirit — you do not receive the Holy Spirit at the time of salvation as many teach! It goes on and says that they laid their hands upon them and they received the Holy Spirit. How did they know that they received it? How did they know that they didn't have it before? There must be a sign so you know for sure that you have received the Holy Spirit. Something so amazing happened to these people that Simon offered the apostles money so that he could also have the power to lay hands on people so that they could receive the Holy Spirit. The next time it happened tells us just what that sign is.

(Acts 10: 44-46)
God told Peter to preach the Gospel at a Gentile's house. Peter didn't want to go because the Jews thought that they were unclean and couldn't be saved. God grabbed Peter by the ear (just about) and made him go. While Peter preached, the Holy Spirit fell on all of the Gentiles there and they received the Holy Spirit. Peter was astonished that they had received the Holy Spirit. The way he knew that they had is because he heard them speaking in tongues! Then he said in verse 47, "Can anyone keep these people from being baptized with water? They have received the Holy Spirit just as we have" SO the way that we can know whether you have received the Holy Spirit is whether or not you speak in tongues.

(Acts 9: 10-18)
Some teach that the Holy Spirit can only come from an apostle. In these verses we see that Ananias was sent by God to pray for Paul so that he could receive the Holy Spirit.

(Acts 19: 1-7)
The last time the Bible recorded that someone received the Holy Spirit is in Ephesus. There Paul met up with some disciples of John. He asked them, "Did you receive the Holy Spirit when you believed?" If you automatically receive the Holy Spirit at the time of salvation then Paul would never have asked such a stupid question. The disciples were taught about Jesus, baptized in his name (so now they are saved) but …

it is only when Paul laid his hands upon them that they received the Holy Spirit. And how did Paul know? He heard them speaking in tongues and prophesying — you don't have to earn the gifts of God or be holy enough — these brand new believers were able to prophesy right away!

So in every case we see that the Holy Spirit is given subsequent to salvation with the evidence of speaking in tongues (usually by the laying on of hands ... if you have not spoken in tongues yet have someone lay hands on you and ask the Holy Spirit to come inside of you). Luke 11: 11-13 states that you have to ask for the Holy Spirit and not worry about receiving a demon (scorpion or snake). Why would Jesus tell us we don't have to worry about receiving a demon when we ask for the Holy Spirit? Because He knew that there would be people who would tell you that speaking in tongues today is of the devil! Shame on them! They are keeping you from the second biggest blessing that God has for you (next to salvation).

I was saved for three years before I found out about the Baptism of the Holy Spirit. During that time I was trying to be good, hoping that I was saved, but to that point nothing supernatural had ever happened to me. I was just going on faith that there was a God and that I was saved. I said that if I spoke in tongues then I would know for sure. One night I went to an Assembly of God Church, the pastor laid his hands on me, and I received the Holy Spirit AND spoke in tongues. I never doubted my salvation after that and I now have a fire in me for God that has never gone out.

Why would you want to speak in tongues? Good question! One day a teenage girl asked me that very question, I told her there are many reasons. First, it is the evidence of receiving the Holy Spirit. None of the Apostles were willing to die for Christ the night of his arrest. These men were cowards (Muslims are willing to die for their religion and soldiers die for their country, but these men were not willing to die for Christ). But something happened to ten of the remaining eleven Apostles ... they gladly died martyrs' deaths. The difference is that the

Holy Spirit changed them into heroes and they received the power to be witnesses for Christ. You can too!

The second reason is that when you speak in tongues you are praying directly to God, perfect prayers from your spirit (I Corinthians: 14: 14). I told that teen that we don't know what to pray for but the Spirit does. I said, "Let's say your best friend is going to be in an accident tomorrow, you don't know that so you don't pray for her and the result is that she dies. Meanwhile, if you prayed in tongues you may pray a prayer that would protect her." She told me that her mother's best friend had died the night before in an automobile accident! I had the thought that if her mother had prayed in tongues she may have prayed a prayer to save her friend's life! Your loved ones need this type of prayer.

Another reason is that it is a miracle. You are speaking in a language you never learned. It could be Greek, Indian, Chinese or even Latin. At a recent prayer meeting I was speaking in tongues and the lady next to be said that I was speaking in Latin. She was a lawyer and had a fair knowledge of Latin. She said that she recognized a number of words that I was speaking.

Next, the Bible tells us that when you speak in an unknown tongue "you edify yourself" (I Corinthians: 14: 4). Now why would you not want to edify yourself? It makes you stronger in the Spirit.

Speaking in tongues is the gateway for the other gifts. (I Corinthians 12: 7-11) It helps the other gifts to flow. And you may have a message in tongues that can be interpreted (I Corinthians 14: 13).

Another reason is that God commands us to eagerly desire spiritual gifts (I Corinthians 14: 1). So obey God and eagerly desire tongues

So speaking in tongues is for today, it is the evidence of receiving the Holy Spirit and it is an essential part of being a Christian (Mark 16: 17). Seek the Holy Spirit with your whole heart and don't stop until you receive it.

# III.  THE BLOOD COVENANT
*(or God is Looking for a Wife!)*

Blood covenants were an important part of the lives of men in Biblical days. There are numerous references made to covenants in the Bible and each gives us a partial glimpse of what a blood covenant is and how it is enacted.

A. **God's Covenant with Abram: Genesis 15: 5-8**
   Abram had just finished a daring rescue of Lot from the kings of the east who had invaded Sodom and Gomorrah. Abram evidently was worried about a counter attack because God came to him in a vision telling him that he would be Abram's shield and great reward. The Lord also made other promises to him and although Abram trusted God concerning his son he asked God for a sign for the other promises.

B. **The Blood Covenant Prepared: Genesis 15: 9-11, 17**
   In answer to Abram's request for a sign that these things are so, God "directed" Abram to make the preparations for a blood covenant. The splitting of the animals was a major point in this blood covenant and Abram was familiar with the ritual involved. The fowls (birds of prey or spiritual buzzards) were demons trying to destroy the covenant before it was even completed.

C. **The Covenant Cut**
   The blood covenant took all day to prepare and soon it was near night. The smoking pot (Jesus?) and blazing torch (Holy Spirit?) are symbolic of God. Man was not allowed to walk through the pieces because this was to be a perfect covenant from God and man would only ruin it by taking part.

D. **The Ritual of the Blood Covenant**
   There are nine steps involved in the fulfillment of a blood covenant:

1. **Exchanging Robes** (I Samuel 18: 1-4)

   The Robes of men in those days were very important ... they gave status as in the purple robes of kings to signify royalty and in the multi-colored coat given to Joseph which made his brothers envious. To exchange coats was to exchange identities with each other. We put on the white linen given to us by Jesus (Revelation 19: 8). God puts on our human flesh, our covering, to become man. When Adam sinned he lost his covering (relationship with God) and tried to cover himself with a fig leaf.

2. **Exchanging Weapons and Belts**

   The belt in those days held all the weapons. By exchanging the belt and weapons each partner swore to defend each other to the death. God has given us all the power and authority He has ... (in the name of Jesus). Jesus said that you will do greater ... (John 14: 12-14). God gets to use us as His servants as His hands, feet and mouth in the physical world magnifying whatever we have.

3. **Cutting the Covenant:** Jeremiah 34: 18-20

   The splitting of the animals in half symbolized that the two halves made up one animal. The two partners will now be made one as the animal once was. It also signifies the death penalty for breaking the covenant since to split the one in half would be to kill it. Jesus became man and God. We have God in us ... the two became one.

4. **Exchanging Names:** Genesis 17: 1-5

   Abram's name was changed to Abraham (... taking the "H" from Yahweh. Later Sarai would also take the "H" and be changed to Sarah). "Abram" means "great father" and "Abraham" means "father of many nations." Jesus was known as the "Son of Man" — and Jesus for the first time referred to God as "Abba" (father), a root word which the name, "Abraham," came from. We are also called "Christians."

5. **Reciting the Covenant Terms and Disclosing of Assets and Debts:** Genesis 17: 6-9
This is a partial list of the terms of the covenant. The two partners would have to disclose every asset and liability they had to the other partner and then recite the terms of the covenant. When we come into a covenant relationship with God we disclose all of our weaknesses (our need for a Savoir, our sins, our inability to be fulfilled without God, etc.) Our assets are our obedience and willingness to serve. God gives us all of His assets; we become joint heirs with Christ (Romans 8: 14-17). We must walk before God and be perfect (through Jesus ... through faith comes righteousness ... Hebrews 11: 12).

6. **Mixing of the Blood**
The two partners would cut each other and let the blood intermingle so that each would have the other's blood running through him. Without the shedding of blood there is no remission of sin (Hebrew 9: 22). "This is my blood of the covenant which is poured out for many" (Mark 14: 24). The Last Supper and every time we celebrate communion we drink the symbolic blood of Jesus and it flows through us. Thus the importance of the blood of Jesus becomes apparent. Without it we cannot have the blood covenant relationship with God that He intended.

7. **Scars:** Genesis 17: 9-11
The scar left on each partner from the mixing of the blood is a constant reminder to them and a warning to potential enemies that they are in a blood covenant. Jesus retained His scars from the cross and showed them to Thomas; this was an eternal reminder to him and to us of our covenant. Circumcision is the scar of the Old Testament for us —

but with the death of Jesus our scars should line up with His — in His hands, in our work; in His feet, in our walk; in His chest, in our hearts. In each of these areas everybody should see a change in their lives or rather a scar where some sin or habit is chopped off. People should be able to look at our scars and know that we are in covenant relationship with Jesus (or rather that we are Christians).

8. **Eat a Memorial Meal:** Genesis 14: 18-20
   Since the blood covenant took all day, part of the ceremony would involve a meal of bread and wine. They would break the loaf in two and drink from the same cup. This is exactly what Jesus has asked us to do in remembrance of Him. Also Revelation 3: 20 states, "If anyone hears my voice and opens the door, I will come in and eat with him, and he with me."

9. **Plant a Memorial Tree**
   This would serve as a reminder for the lives of the two partners that on that spot the covenant was made. They would also sprinkle it with blood of sacrificed animals. Jesus, at his last act on Earth, planted a memorial tree that still serves as a reminder of our covenant and He sprinkled the cross (tree) with His blood.

Adam was in a covenant relationship with God before the fall. He was covered with the robe of righteousness of God. He had power and dominion over the entire world (granted to him by God). When Eve was made the covenant was cut (Adam's rib and the shedding and mingling of blood with Eve). Adam was given his name by God. The terms of the covenant were stated: Adam was not to eat of the tree of knowledge of good and evil but was allowed to eat of all the others. The tree of life was the memorial tree planted (it will still be in Heaven for eternity states Revelation 22: 2). When Adam broke the covenant the penalty was death.

The covenant with Abraham applies to all of us. He is the father of us all … (Romans 4: 16-17). "As it is written I have made you a father of many nations." The purpose of the blood covenant was to bring us up to a level where we would be a suitable bride for Christ. Only with God in us, with the blood of Jesus shed for our sins. With the robes of righteousness and our scars are we to be that spotless bride that He will come back for.

Marriage is also a blood covenant. The woman takes on the man's name. All assets and debts are shared. The two become one flesh. The wedding banquet is the memorial meal. The vows include the words, "to death do us part," and most importantly the hymen is broken and blood is shed! No other animal has a hymen. God created the hymen in women for only one purpose … the wedding night and the blood covenant.

# IV. THE FIVE BIG WHYS

These questions have perplexed man for thousands of years. The greatest minds in the world have pondered these questions with little success. Although the Bible does not come right out and clearly answer these questions in a direct way it does give us enough information to make some logical conclusions. Other doctrines such as the Trinity and the Rapture also require some deduction so this is permissible.

**Question #1: Why did God create a material world?**

For untold eons of time there existed only the spiritual world (as far as we know). This spiritual world consisted of a multitude of angels, all of whom praised and worshipped God. Then, all of a sudden, God decided to create another plane of existence in which the spiritual world has access to us but we have little or no access to it. The following time line demonstrates the enormity of this question.

"In the beginning God created the
Heavens and the Earth." Genesis 1: 1

"Then I saw a new Heaven and a new Earth
for the first Earth had passed away ... I
saw the new Jerusalem coming down from
Heaven." Revelation 21: 1-2

So the question is why create a material world, allow it to exist for a fraction of time (in relation to eternity) and then destroy it and put its inhabitants into the spiritual world and never have a material world again?

66

# Question #2: Why was man created?

Most denominations state that man was created to give glory to God, to worship God ... or for God who is a creative being to express Himself by creating (much like an artist but even though He hasn't sold a painting He continues to paint). Others state that man was made so that God could share His love with them. All of these speculations are true but none of them completely satisfy the question.

Angels were made to give glory to God, to worship Him and so that God could share His love with them. Why did God need to do the same thing in another plane of existence? As far as God being a creative being, although this is true, it doesn't explain why He would create a material world then destroy it, never to have it exist again. Something must have happened in the spiritual world that would make God want to create this world and man in particular. This brings us to question #3.

# Question #3: Why does God allow Satan to go unpunished?

Satan held a very high place in the Kingdom of God before his fall. (Ezekiel 28: 13-15) He was perfect in all of his ways until iniquity was found in him. God had three choices when Satan rebelled ...

1. **Punish Satan immediately.** If God did this, all the remaining faithful angels would start to fear that God would destroy them if they ever stepped out of line. They would start to obey God out of fear instead of love. This would lead to resentment and eventually to hate.

2. **Do nothing.** God couldn't allow the situation to continue because already one third of the angels were following Satan (Revelation 12: 4). Without any rules chaos would follow just as it does here on Earth. Also God is a just god and justice must be done.

3. **Delay punishment.** This is the wisest course to take. Since Satan was either never offered mercy or more likely refused it when offered God never had the opportunity in history to show that He was a merciful and loving God.

So God created another world in which He placed a creature known as man. Man was created lower than angels (Hebrews 2: 7), and put into an environment where he will freely sin. All that these lowly, sinful men had to do to obtain mercy was to repent and make Jesus their Lord. The angels are intently interested in the whole salvation process (I Peter 1: 10-12). They can't understand why God would leave His throne and suffer at the hands of these lowly creatures.

Satan (and man) will be judged, but not until the material world is done away with. God did not want to show His wrath until He was ready to show His mercy.

The reason why God created a material world was first, because it put man in a lower and more restraining position than angels. If God could show mercy to this lowly creature then surely He would show it to the higher creation also. Second, we can sin down here with less harm to the Kingdom of God. To be in the presence of God and willfully sin is an insult to the Creator. Third, the angels can watch as spectators without interfering with their presence being known. If we saw the demons that are whispering those horrible thoughts into our ears we wouldn't give them the same consideration that we do when we think that those thoughts are our own.

## Question #4: Why does God allow Satan to torment man?

(Job 2: 1-10) We see in the story of Job that Satan has free access to God. He is allowed to accuse man day and night (Revelation 12: 10) and torment him with sickness, unrest and death. Satan is like a roaring lion looking for someone to devour (I Peter 5: 8). Why is Satan so interested in doing this to us? The answer is threefold. First, in Job, the whole question is whether God is worthy of unmerited love or not. Will man still love God even if God doesn't do a thing for him? Second, Satan is mad. Revelation 12: 12 says, "But woe to the earth and the sea, because the devil has gone down to you! He is filled with fury because he knows that his time is short." Third, Satan accuses the brethren because he is trying to convince God that not one man deserves mercy. If he is successful in this then God won't be able to demonstrate His mercy to man and He won't be able to punish Satan! Satan wants back what he feels is rightly his.

The question remains why God allows him to do it. That will be answered with the next question.

## Question #5: Why do Christians suffer?

I can understand why God would allow unrepentant sinners to suffer, but why His children? God created pain as a warning device so if you accidentally touch a hot stove you feel pain, remove your hand before it is seriously burnt. When you feel pain you know something is wrong and you attempt to find out what to do about it. Pain motivates you into action. God allows Satan to torment us so that we will feel pain (both physical and emotional). When we feel this pain God wants us to turn to Him to seek relief from the pain. He uses pain in the unbeliever to bring him to Christ and in the believer to produce growth.

God allows Satan to cause us pain so that when he is judged he will have no excuse (like he attempted with Job ... the accusation being that we only love God for the things He does not for who He is). All of creation will see that millions of men have turned to God regardless of pain, suffering and even loss of life. When we come to Christ we give him everything (he already owns it all anyway — we just think we do). Without suffering loss and pain there is no real test of our love for God. To make the situation fair God, Himself, gave up everything (much more than we ever had) and came down in the form of Jesus as a man to suffer much more than we ever will and finally die for us. Never can we be mad at God for allowing pain in our life when He suffered it right along with us.

(Revelation 21: 24-27) The purpose of this material world and our suffering here is that God will not allow anyone into Heaven who will defile it. That is the purpose of the thousand year reign of Jesus here on Earth. During this time He will rule with a rod of iron. We will have to grow during this time so that when Satan is loosed again (Revelation 20: 7) we will decide for Christ. Growing means that we surrender more of our will over to the Lord and become more like Him.

# V. YOU CAN PROPHESY

There have been many books written encouraging you to prophesy but I have yet to see one that tells you how to do it. It is rather simple. I'll get to "the how-to" in a few minutes, but first I want to explain why you should *want* to.

First, Paul tells the Corinthians, "Follow the way of love and eagerly desire spiritual gifts, especially the gift of prophecy" (I Corinthians 14: 1). Why would he tell us to desire that gift even more than miracles, or healing? The answer I think is because the gift of prophecy is a direct word from God to that person. What could be more important than that? We need to hear from God on a regular basis. In a prophecy there is usually comfort, strengthening, and encouragement (I Corinthians 14:3). Often the only words we hear from God comes from the Sunday morning sermon which often tells us that we are dirty rotten sinners and here is a twelve step program to overcome that sin. The prophecy may also have words of knowledge (a word telling you something that the person giving the prophecy would have no way of knowing … i.e., your address or middle name etc.) This is so that you will know he is hearing from God and not just making the prophecy up. Don't we need to hear from God beyond what He speaks privately to us? Often the prophecy confirms something that God has already told us. Sometimes it will tell us something we wouldn't hear from God ourselves because we would have shut it off because we didn't want to do whatever the prophecy says.

So, God commands us to eagerly desire the gifts … especially prophecy.

Second, we should want to prophesy because it builds up the body of Christ (I Corinthians 14: 12). A prophetic word edifies the Church. What church would want to discourage being edified?

The third reason is because prophecy is the sign of the End Time Church. The gifts and callings of God had almost vanished for 1500 years because the Catholic Church didn't understand or allow the gifts to operate. Slowly over the last several hundred years, however, the gifts have been creeping back into the Church. Martin Luther reintroduced the gift of faith which started the Protestant Reformation. The gift of tongues started flowing at the start of the twentieth century with the Azusa Street revival. The gifts of healing were big in the 1950's. Prophecy has become more and more used in the past twenty years. Peter quotes the prophet, Joel.

(Act 2: 17-18)
> [17]*In the last days, God says, I will pour out my Spirit on all people. Your sons and daughters will prophesy, your young men will see visions, your old men will dream dreams.*
> [18]*Even on my servants, both men and women, I will pour out my Spirit in those days, and they will prophesy.*

Something needs to change in our churches to allow our children and others to prophesy. First, why does every message, no matter the topic, have to be an hour long? In the letter to the Ephesians, Paul teaches on predestination, prayer, oneness with Christ, unity in the body of Christ, marriage, the armor of God, and a whole host of other topics all in ten minutes. If our pastors cut their messages in half and allowed the remaining time for prophecy the Church would benefit greatly.

There is only one place in the Bible where a church service is described. I Corinthians 14: 26-33 tells us that everyone can prophesy so that everyone may be instructed and encouraged. Almost every prophecy I've ever heard is only a few minutes or less long. God can use everybody in the Church to instruct, encourage, edify, and strengthen us.

I've seen eight year old kids prophesy with such wisdom it was astounding. But the only way that it is going to happen is if the people are encouraged, taught how to prophesy and given the opportunity to do so. You need to have small groups. (It would be impossible for a child to prophesy for the first time on a Sunday morning in front of hundreds of people. I had a hard time doing it with years of experience!) You also can break up the Sunday morning meeting into small groups and have a leader in each group who will encourage the others to prophesy. Since many people will only attend church on Sunday that is the only way they will ever use their gifts.

The body has many parts and each person has a gift. For the most part the only gifts that our churches will allow is for people to be Sunday school teachers, or deacons (to clean up), or ushers. Few are ever allowed to hear from God and share what He tells them. But if you want to be the fulfillment of the prophecy given by Joel you're going to have to encourage the gift of prophecy!

Now it's time to teach you how to prophesy. Paul says that if you speak in an unknown tongue pray that you may interpret what you are saying. I tell people to pray in tongues and ask God for the interpretation. While they are praying in tongues a few words will come into their mind in English. Usually God will only give you a few words to start (if he gave you the entire message you would forget it or mess it up). Once you get those few words (they will sound like your own thoughts), speak them out and keep on talking in English without thinking of what to say (like you do with tongues).

*One time a gigantic lady came into my store. She must have weighed 400 pounds! I got to talking to her and asked her if she would like to receive the Holy Spirit with the evidence of speaking in tongues. She said she would. I told her that the Holy Spirit would come and live within her and that she would receive power from Him. She was excited. But, I told her that first I wanted to prophesy over her (I always like to whenever I minister to people). I prayed in tongues and the four words I got were, "You are a whale." I thought to myself that it must be the devil because it couldn't be God! I tested the Spirit (I John 4:1). I asked the spirit if Jesus came in the flesh — he said, "Yes." But I still was not willing to say what seemed to be an outrageous insult. I asked God to give me something else instead of that. He said, "No." I then asked that He give me the next line of the prophecy. He said, "No." So after five minutes of sweating I finally got up the nerve and told her God says, "You are a whale!" I didn't know what I was going to say next but without thinking out came, "... and just as the whale swallowed Jonah so will you swallow the Holy Spirit. And just as Jonah was able to think and live within the whale so will the Holy Spirit live within you." I was amazed that God gave such a profound word to her. I asked her if she was offended and she assured me that she thought it was funny and that she would always remember that prophecy.*

So people, let's open up our churches and let the prophecy flow!

# VI. SICKNESS AND DELIVERANCE

Sometimes when Jesus met up with a person who was sick He cast a demon out of them. Some diseases may be caused by a demon and if the demon is cast out often times the person is healed. In the past year we had four people who were diagnosed with cancer (x-rays to prove it) and with no treatment whatsoever they were healed just by casting out a demon.

*A thirty year old doctor had been diagnosed with breast cancer in both breasts. The x-rays revealed lumps that appeared to be cancerous. She was told she would have to undergo extensive chemotherapy and radiation treatments. She really didn't want to do that so she called me up. I went over to her house and prayed for God to heal her. The next week she went for more x-rays and the cancer was still there. She called me again and this time told me that both her mother and grandmother had lost both of their breasts from cancer. I realized that this was a generational curse. I broke the curse over her and then commanded the cancer demons to leave her. She felt them come out of her breasts and leave! Next I called out rebellious spirits and they also left.*

*I was getting tired and I told her to come to the next meeting because she needed fifteen minutes more deliverance. She then went for her next set of x-rays a few days later and the doctors were amazed that the tumors had shrunk dramatically and no longer appeared cancerous! Did she come to the next meeting to finish up? Noooooo! I didn't see her again for four months. During that time she never returned to the doctor. She just wanted to believe that she was healed and didn't want to think about it any more.*

*When she finally came to another meeting she told me the only reason why she came that night was because her four year old daughter had wanted to visit me that evening. I hadn't spoken more than twelve words to this little girl in my whole life and had not seen her for four months. Her mother was puzzled and asked her why she had said she wanted to see me. She told her mom, "Jesus told me to say that!" That was the only time she had ever said anything like that, so her mom got into the car and came to the meeting. That night we finished casting out the remaining demons. A few days latter she went for x-rays and they were absolutely clear. Not a sign of tumors or cancer!*

Did you notice that I cast out both spirits of cancer and rebellion? Many diseases are caused by our sins. When we think thoughts often chemicals are released to prepare us for whatever action we may need to take. Fear will cause adrenalin to be released. Worry will cause stomach acids to be released and so on. Here are a few sins and the sicknesses that can be associated with them. When doing deliverance break the generational curses and cast out the demons of both the sickness and the sin.

- Cancer: rebellion and bitterness.
- Heart problems: fear.
- PMS: fear pf pain, feelings of sexual uncleanness.
- Migraines: guilt and fear.
- Ovarian cysts, breast cysts: conflict with mother.
- Acne: fear of man (peer pressure).
- Arthritis: unforgiveness.
- Ulcers: worry
- Auto-immune disease: self-hatred.

Obsessive-compulsive cleaning can be caused by a hormone that mothers release right before they have a baby. This hormone causes the 'nesting instinct' and often the pregnant mother will compulsively clean her house so the baby will be safe. An example in nature may be that of a bird who meticulously builds a nest in the spring for its babies. This behavior can also be caused by a spirit of fear — either fear of your child getting sick or fear of you getting sick.

The 'nesting instinct' is related to the hormone that causes a new mother to be protective of her new baby. Most mothers would gladly die to protect their baby from harm. We see this behavior in animals, e.g., a mother bear will kill anyone that comes between her and her cubs and a mother dog who normally will never hurt anyone will bite someone who touches her puppies. A demon can cause these hormones to be released bringing about weird behaviors in people. You often have to find the exact cause of the problem and the related chemical interaction that it is having on the body. Psychiatrists prescribe millions of doses of psychogenic drugs claiming that their patients have a brain chemistry imbalance. Well they do have a brain chemistry imbalance but it's not from a physical malfunction. It is because they are thinking negative thoughts all day long and the brain releases negative chemicals. Change the way you think ... renew your mind and your chemistry will be back in balance. Cast out the demons that are putting those thoughts there and you won't need a psychiatrist!

(Philippians 4: 8)

> *8Finally, brothers, whatever is true, whatever is noble, whatever is right, whatever is pure, whatever is lovely, whatever is admirable — if anything is excellent or praiseworthy — think about such things.*

# VII. THE END TIME CHURCH

What direction should our churches be heading? Should we seek mega-churches that have the most charismatic teachers, best worship music, and best services for our family, or the smaller church where you become a part of the church family, getting to know everyone and becoming a part of their lives. Or should the Church evolve into something else and if so what? The Bible has the answer for us!

Today our Protestant churches are run just about the same way throughout the world. It doesn't matter whether you are in Brazil or Russia or China or the USA; we almost always do the same thing. We sing five songs (three fast ones then two slow ones); we then take up the collection (where we are told that we don't give enough money). Then the pastor talks about God for an hour — longer or shorter depending on the church but almost always the fully allotted time. Then that's it! Everybody goes home and says, "Wow, that was a really good service." Fifty years from now you will still be sitting in the pew hearing the man talk about God ... for some of you three times a week. Aren't you getting sick of just hearing about God? Wouldn't you rather experience Him instead of hearing how somebody else did four thousand years ago? What our church services should be doing is allowing people to experience God. But after the hour long teaching everybody is bored and tired and ready to go home. There is no time for anything else and the next meeting will be exactly the same except the title of the sermon will be different.

Why does every message, no matter the topic, always have to be an hour or more long? Paul teaches in the letter to the Ephesians on prayer, unity, Christian living, marriage, children, slaves and masters, and the armor of God, all in ten minutes. Almost every prophecy from God is just a few minutes long. God knows our attention span is less than ten minutes and He keeps His teachings short. Why don't we?

What was the early Church service like? There is only one place in the entire Bible that tells us about their services and it was nothing like our meetings today. In I Corinthians 14: 26-32 Paul asks us ...

> *26What then shall we say, brothers? When you come together, everyone has a hymn, or a word of instruction, a revelation, a tongue or an interpretation. All of these must be done for the strengthening of the church.*
> *27If anyone speaks in a tongue, two--or at the most three--should speak, one at a time, and someone must interpret.*
> *28If there is no interpreter, the speaker should keep quiet in the church and speak to himself and God.*
> *29Two or three prophets should speak, and the others should weigh carefully what is said.*
> *30And if a revelation comes to someone who is sitting down, the first speaker should stop.*
> *31For you can all prophesy in turn so that everyone may be instructed and encouraged.*
> *32The spirits of prophets are subject to the control of prophets.*

So in the early Church everybody heard from God! Some would bring in songs to sing, others would bring teachings (a word, not an hour-long sermon), people would get revelations about God ... there would be two or three people getting messages in tongues, someone (or several people) would interpret. There would also be several people who would prophesy. Paul says that you may *all* prophesy so that you may *all* "learn and be comforted!" Much of the teaching in this church would come through the prophetic word! Everybody was encouraged to share what God was telling them during the service. They were taught and given the opportunity to hear from God (what Church does that today — not many!)

Notice there is no mention of the pastor! The word is only mentioned scant few times in the Bible yet today he is the only indispensable member of the Church. None of the letters to the churches in the New Testament are addressed to the pastor. All of them are addressed to the elders, the brethren, the church, or the saints. When Paul wrote to Titus (Titus 1: 5) he instructed him to appoint elders in every town. Paul also told Timothy what the qualifications for a deacon and an elder were. Notice that elders were appointed but pastors were not. The qualifications for the most important office in today's church, the office of pastor, aren't even discussed!

When Paul, Timothy and Titus started churches they would go into a town and spend several months getting people saved and then they would leave and come back at a latter time to appoint elders. Who would they appoint? Would they appoint men who monopolized the meetings and refused to allow anyone except a select few to speak or would they choose men who knew that the body of Christ consisted of many parts and everyone was important in the functioning of the Church. Men were appointed because they allowed everyone to take part in the service and because they encouraged each to use their gifts and taught them how to do so.

Nowhere in the Bible are we told to have a church service like what we have today. So where did it come from? I think that for the first hundred or so years it was like the Corinth Church. Slowly, however, since people are lazy and would rather just sit and do nothing and that because some men like to rule and monopolize we started moving away from the early church model. When the Catholic Church dominated the Christian community only the priest was allowed to talk and hear from God. In the 1500's Martin Luther and Calvin started bringing back Biblical truths but it wasn't until the twentieth century that the gifts of the Holy Spirit were back in operation in the Church. After a hundred years aren't we ready now to really let them move in the Church?

I'm not faulting our churches of today and I'm not saying that they don't do a lot of good. But I think we can do better! The Bible tells us what the End Time Church is going to look like. Peter quotes the prophet Joel:

80

(Acts 2: 17-18)

> [17] *In the last days, God says, I will pour out my Spirit on all people. Your sons and daughters will prophesy, your young men will see visions, your old men will dream dreams.*
> [18] *Even on my servants, both men and women, I will pour out my Spirit in those days, and they will prophesy.*

He tells us that in the last days He will pour out his Spirit on your sons and daughters — your young men, your old men, even the servants both men and women. Notice it is all the people in the Church ... your children, servants, old men, even the women! He doesn't say your pastors and bishops will prophesy or that the elders will have visions but the little people. How can this come about in the churches of today? Even in the best of churches you may only have three or four prophecies in a meeting. That means in a church of 500 it would take 125 weeks before everyone had a chance to prophesy even once. It is also so hard to prophesy in a big group setting that the insignificant people would be so overwhelmed that they would never open their mouths. The only way it could happen is in a small group setting where the people are given the absolute freedom to try out their gifts, where they are taught how to hear from God. It can happen in every church — you just need someone to show you how. Our pastors are selected on one major basis; if people are willing to come and hear him talk about God for an hour he can be a pastor. So, for the most part, our pastors don't always have the gift of pastoring but rather a gift of teaching. Everybody knows that a teacher wants to talk; they don't want to listen (remember high school).

So the End Time Church should be like the Corinth Church where everybody took part. In the large churches of today I encourage the pastors to cut their messages short to allow ample time for prophecy. They should also make small group meetings mandatory for all members. At each meeting they should ask first time visitors to stand and say where they are from and instruct the small group leader of that area to introduce himself and invite him to his home meeting. With the proper training every church can really start moving in the gifts of the

Holy Spirit. Instead of just the pastor or elders or guest speaker ministering, it will be everyone in the congregation!

I've had eight year old kids prophesy better than I. I have seen thirteen year old girls who were just saved moments before cast out demons and hundreds of people who never had been exposed to the gifts of the Holy Spirit come to their first meeting and prophecy or cast out demons or heal the sick. You don't have to be a "mature" Christian to use the gifts — look at the Corinth Church; they were all messed up. You just have to have willing leaders, small settings (10-25 people) and people who know how to encourage and release the body into their giftings.

# VIII. THE END TIME AND THE WORLD TRADE CENTER

People often ask me why they should believe in the Bible. I tell them that there are many reasons. The most important ones to me are that the Bible is filled with prophecies that have already come true, others that are to come about in the future and some that are being fulfilled in our lifetimes! Take a look at Revelation, chapters 17 and 18.

(Revelation 17: 1-2)

> ¹*One of the seven angels who had the seven bowls came and said to me, "Come, I will show you the punishment of the great prostitute, who sits on many waters.*
> ²*With her the kings of the earth committed adultery and the inhabitants of the earth were intoxicated with the wine of her adulteries.*

(Revelation 18: 2-5)

> ²*Fallen! Fallen is Babylon the Great! She has become a home for demons and a haunt for every evil spirit …*
> ³*For all the nations have drunk the maddening wine of her adulteries. The kings of the earth committed adultery with her and the merchants of the earth grew rich from her excessive luxuries.*
> ⁴*Then I heard another voice from heaven say: Come out of her my people, so that you will not share in her sins, so that you will not receive any of her plagues;*
> ⁵*For her sins are piled up to heaven.*

If we are in the end times then there is a place in existence today that will fit this description: There is only one country in the world where all the merchants of the world are growing rich from this particular country's excessive luxuries. This country has become a dwelling place for demons. The fact that it has *become* a dwelling place means at one time it was not possessed by demons. There are also Christians in this country ... *"come out of her my people."* It is a place where all the nations have drunk the wine of her impure passion.

It seems that only the United States fits the bill. In 1960, over 600 movies were made, every one of them are "G" rated. Now, only 6 out of 600 movies made are "G" rated. Our music is now filled with profanity, sex and violence. Our TV shows once were wholesome but are now filled with every perversion known to man. All the nations of the world want our music, TV shows, and movies ... *"they have drunk the wine of her impure passion."* No matter where in the world you go you will see the American culture and it is not good! We are spreading sin throughout the world and enjoying the excessive luxury from the profits.

The United States sits on many waters; the Atlantic on one side, the Pacific on the other, the Great Lakes and Bering Sea to the north and the Gulf of Mexico to the south. We are almost an island nation.

Abortion was made legal along with pornography and homosexual marriage, all thanks to Democratic judges who imposed their lack of morality on our nation! I believe that we are one of the first nations in the history of mankind to legalize homosexual marriages. Decades ago Billy Graham said that if God didn't judge New York City for its sin then God would have to apologize to Sodom and Gomorrah. I think our time of judgment is coming and, perhaps, it has already started. The Bible tells us what that punishment will be.

(Revelation 18: 9-11)
> [9]*When the kings of the earth who committed adultery with her and shared her luxury see the smoke of her burning, they will weep and mourn over her.*
> [10]*Terrified at her torment, they will stand far off and cry: Woe! Woe, O great city, O Babylon, city of power! In one hour your doom has come!*
> [11]*The merchants of the earth will weep and mourn over her because no one buys their cargoes any more ...*

(Revelation 18: 17-19)

> [17]*In one hour such great wealth has been brought to ruin! Every sea captain, and all who travel by ship … will stand far off.*
>
> [18]*When they see the smoke of her burning, they will exclaim, Was there ever a city like this great city?*
>
> [19]*They will throw dust on their heads, and with weeping and mourning cry out: Woe!, O great city, where all who had ships on the sea became rich through her wealth! In one hour she has been brought to ruin!*

These verses tell us that we are now talking about a great city, unlike any other city that ever existed. What is the greatest city on the face of the earth? New York City, of course!

How long did it take for the World Trade Center towers to fall? ONE HOUR! As we discussed before, the United States is almost an island nation and anything not made in Canada or Mexico is brought to us by ship. That is why the scripture mentions that all who trade on the sea will weep and mourn.

The most amazing thing is that the buildings were called the World Trade Center … "*all the nations of the* **world** *who* **traded**" …! The Bible almost mentions the buildings by name.

What do you remember the most about 9-11? The smoke coming from the buildings … "*the smoke of her burning.*" What city has the most luxurious lifestyle? New York!

Perhaps, for the first time ever, all the nations of the earth wept and mourned for the United States … "*all the kings of the earth … will weep and mourn.*"

Often times, in Bible prophecy, there is a partial fulfillment and then later on the completion of the prophecy. A good example is in Acts 2 when Peter quotes the Prophet Joel.

(Acts 2: 17, 20)

> *17In the last days, God says, I will pour out my spirit on all people.*
> *Your sons and daughters will prophesy, and your young men shall*
> *see visions, and your old men shall dream dreams;*
>
> *20The sun will be turned to darkness and the moon to blood before*
> *the great and glorious day of the Lord comes.*

In the first part Peter is claiming the prophecy to be, at least, partially fulfilled in his time, but before the coming of the Lord there will be a completion. Perhaps, there will be a future, more complete fulfillment of Revelation 18 where New York City will be hit again.

The sad thing is that after 9-11 many Americans turned to God ... but not in repentance. The prevalent attitude was "God Bless America." We wanted to be blessed! There were only two TV preachers who claimed that God was punishing America for our sins and to their shame, both recanted after intense media pressure. Both Pat Robertson and Jerry Falwell said they made a mistake and didn't mean that 9-11 was a token of God's wrath. If this was God's judgment on America we certainly did not repent. Since then we legalized homosexual marriages and have taken many more steps away from God. Then we have the nerve to ask God to bless us!

# IX.   THE END TIME AND "666"

(Revelation 13: 1, 7, 16-18)
> *¹And I saw a beast coming out of the sea ...*

> *⁷He was given power to make war against the saints and to conquer them. And he was given authority over every tribe, people, language and nation.*

> *¹⁶He also forced everyone, small and great, rich and poor, free and slave, to receive a mark on his right hand or on his forehead,*
> *¹⁷So that no one could buy or sell unless he has the mark, which is the name of the beast or the number of his name.*
> *¹⁸This calls for wisdom. If anyone has insight, let him calculate the number of the beast, for it is man's number. His number is 666.*

These passages from Revelation 13 point to us presently being in the end times. John tells us that there will be one man who will rule the earth and that nobody will be able to buy or sell unless he has a mark on his hand or forehead. He tells us that this calls for wisdom, so it won't be evident. He also tells us that this mark will be a number and the number is 666.

Today we have a system of buying and selling that is in place in almost every store in the nation and it relies on marks which are numbers. It is the UPC code and it is on almost everything you buy. The UPC code consists of a series of marks or bars that represent numbers. These bars are scanned by a computer hooked up to store cash registers.

Every bar code has three guard bars. These bars tell the computer where to begin reading, where the middle is, and where the bar code ends. Every two lines in a bar code stand for a number, and as you can see in the graphic on the next page, the three guard bars are the same. Guess what number those two lines represent? You guessed it; it is the number 6. How do we know this? Look at the number 6 on the code;

directly above it is the same two lines that are in the guard bars. So every UPC code has the number 666 in it!

The Bible tells us we will be required to have a mark which is a number and the number is 666! Some time in the near future you will be forced to have your social security number put on your hand in the form of a UPC code. Each social security number will have to have the 6, 6, 6 marks to guide the computer. Maybe it will be because of criminal activity in the form of identity theft, counterfeiting, stolen credit cards, or some other scheme, that your hand will have to be imprinted with your identity number in order to stop these crimes. You will not be able to buy or sell unless you have this mark on your hand. Cash, credit cards and checks will be done away with.

Revelation 13: 18 says this calls for wisdom. You have been using UPC codes most of your life and you probably never knew that they had 666 incorporated into them. The UPC code was developed under a government contract by a couple of Harvard graduate students. They were the ones who chose 6, 6, 6, to be on every code. They may have done it unwittingly or as a prank, knowing what Scripture says. Whatever their reason it will be used to fulfill Bible prophecy.

In 2001, there was a man who controlled every person in the world's ability to buy or sell. Who was that man? President Bush! After 9-11 he froze the bank accounts of everybody he named as a terrorist throughout the world! Even Swiss banks cooperated for the first time in history. They had never allowed any government to interfere with their secret bank accounts ever before.

Obviously, President Bush is not the anti-Christ and what he did was a good thing, but it set the stage for the evil one to do the same thing. The difference, however, will be that the anti-Christ will also control Christians and freeze their bank accounts unless they renounce Christ.

What will you do when you are told to take the mark? It may seem innocent or it may be that you have to renounce your belief in order to even buy food. I hope that you will refuse the mark because Revelation 20:4 says that those who do not take the mark and are slain will be risen up and reign with Christ for a thousand years.

# PARCIQG ChOUGHCS

*I know that some of the teachings in this book may be new to some of you. I can assure you that I have personally tested each of the teachings and found them to be true. I am amazed by the feedback from many of the readers on how this book has changed their lives. When they try to give me the credit I just tell them that these teachings are not mine; every one of these teachings has a scriptural foundation in the Bible.*

*The teachings in this book have shown hundreds of people how to be set free from drug addictions, depression, psychotic disorders, demonic oppression, physical disease, and a whole host of other ailments. I pray that you will be open to let God heal you too! I am always ready to help, no matter what the problem. You may contact me at the Mustard Seed Christian Bookstore in Waterbury, Ct. or call me at 203-754-3994.*

*Remember the most important teaching in this book is that God loves you and He didn't create you just to constantly condemn you. He created you to have a loving Father/child relationship. All you have to do is receive it and believe it. LOVE, Ray.*

Made in the USA
Las Vegas, NV
04 December 2021

36114204R00056